THROUGH THE CONCRETE

A Memoir of Breaking Through Barriers, Reclaiming Faith, and Becoming Whole

Briana Cobb

Publisher Branch & Bloom Publishing

Paperback ISBN: 979-8-9994787-1-9

Hard cover ISBN: 979-8-9994787-0-2

Ebook ISBN: 979-8-9994787-2-6

Cover and Interior Design by:

Deborah Perdue, Illumination Graphics

Dedication

To my children —

your love has been the soil in which I continue to grow. You are my reason, my rhythm, and my reminder to keep going.

To my parents —

gone too soon, yet forever present in the roots of who I am. I honor the life you gave me, the lessons, the pain, and the resilience.

To God —

I return this offering to You. Thank You for never leaving me, for providing, protecting, revealing, and refining me. For seeing me when I couldn't see myself, and for allowing my life to become a vessel — one that empowers, uplifts, and gives hope to others.

Acknowledgments

This book would not exist without the support, encouragement, and divine alignment of so many incredible souls.

To my writing coach, Elizabeth Ann Atkins — thank you for helping me unearth my voice, guiding me with patience and power, and reminding me that my story matters.

To my graphic designer, Deborah Perdue — your creative gifts brought my vision to life with grace and beauty. Your work gave this message a face.

To my uncle, Trap — Leonard Seale— my first mentor. You taught me how to fish instead of giving me one, setting me on the path of financial literacy and self-sufficiency. Thank you for believing in my ability to stand on my own and for being a steady example of wisdom, survival, and grit.

To Melvenna Fant-Jones, founder of the nonprofit WHEAT — your heart, strength, and spirit have left a lasting mark on my life. Your unwavering generosity, radiant positivity, and commitment to uplifting others inspire me daily. I thank God for your example and the light you shine in this world.

To my family and friends — your love, prayers, and presence sustained me. I'm forever grateful for every word of encouragement and every quiet moment of support.

To those who came before me, those who poured into me, and those who will be changed by this story — this is for you.

To my husband Daryl Cobb Jr. —
Thank you for being a part of my story. Your presence, even through challenges, has played a role in shaping the woman I've become. Navigating fears and traumas — both mine and yours — and overcoming them over these years has been nothing short of the evidence of God's grace and power to sustain. I am forever grateful for the partner you are in helping raise our children and care for our home, especially throughout the process of writing this book. Thank you for your resources and subtle guidance, even as you faced and healed through your own storms. I'm especially thankful for the moments of laughter we've shared — reminders of the value of friendship, and the simple joy in choosing to be present with one another.

To my former therapist, Michelle Myers — thank you for seeing me, truly. For treating me like a whole human being when I felt fragmented and unseen. You gave me a reference point. Your dedication to my healing, your willingness to advocate for me, and your commitment to helping me get the right diagnosis changed the trajectory of my life. You gave me tools, language, and safety. You reminded me that I wasn't broken — I was blooming. I'll never forget the day you shared your vision of me growing like a flower. That image lives in these pages, and in every part of the woman I've become.

And ultimately, to God — the Source of it all. Thank You for carrying me, revealing me to myself, and allowing my life to be used as a vessel to remind others who they truly are in connection to you.

Content Note:

This memoir contains themes of childhood trauma, emotional neglect, spiritual conditioning, parental loss, and references to suicide.

While these moments are written with care and honesty, they may be difficult for some readers. If you find yourself needing to pause or step away, please honor that. Your well-being comes first.

This story is not shared to retraumatize, but to offer connection, healing, and truth. I have added some rooted reflections at the end of each section to help you pause and breathe as we navigate this hand in hand. You will learn, it's ok to be vulnerable and it's ok to release.

You are not alone.

Prologue:

I didn't want to write a book.
I wanted a million dollars.

I remember the moment I said it out loud. It was less of a wish and more of a prayer disguised as a plan. I wasn't kneeling or lighting candles—I was just a tired mom, sitting in the mess of life, soul-searching. And I asked:

"God, show me how to make a million dollars. I want to build generational wealth. I want to change my life."

I meant it from a pure place.
I wanted freedom for my children. I wanted options. I wanted to undo years of survival and finally taste what ease might feel like.

I had come to see God as a giver of things—like a divine genie. My prayers were mostly transactional: "Ask and you shall receive." It wasn't intimacy I was seeking—it was relief. That mindset, I realize now, wasn't entirely my fault. It came from how I was raised, from how life had taught me to survive. I didn't yet know what a real relationship with God could look like. But the truth? I was being guided all along.
Quietly protected.

God was waiting patiently for me to see differently.

I had just begun learning about wealth building, and everything I studied pointed to the same truth: if you want financial freedom, you need assets. You need capital. You need a strategy.

And in my mind, the number that stuck was.... **a million**.

But what I was really asking for—beneath the dollars and data—was something deeper: **security, freedom, a clean slate, and legacy**.

I expected an answer like *real estate* or *a business plan* or *investments*.

Instead, I kept hearing one word:
Book.

Not blueprint.
Not budget.
Book.

At first, I resisted. I questioned it. Prayed again. But the answer didn't change.

Write the book Briana.

It was frustrating. Confusing.
Kind of like telling your child to take their medicine when they don't understand why. They trust you, but only up to the point where understanding hasn't caught up with obedience. That's how I felt.

I trusted God—but I didn't yet understand the assignment.
Still, the more I resisted, the more things aligned.
People showed up.

Resources appeared.
Ideas, coaches, nudges, synchronicities—it felt like something
had already been set in motion, waiting for me to surrender.

So, I began writing.
Reluctantly at first.
But as the words came, so did the healing.

What started as a pursuit of financial wealth became a journey
toward wholeness.
I thought I was chasing money—
But God was offering me freedom.
A deeper relationship.
A restored identity.
A healed past.
A hope-filled future.

This book wasn't born out of ambition, but surrender.
And I'm writing it for you.
To show you that it's okay to question the path.
To want one thing and receive what you truly need.
To begin again—without shame.

I'm writing to help you pause.
To become an observer.
Because when you begin to examine your patterns, beliefs,
and emotional inheritance, you stop judging yourself—and
something sacred opens:

You realize you have a choice.
To participate or not.
To stay in the pattern or break it.

To live the story you inherited—or write a new one.

That's how we begin to create our reality.

I want to show you how my relationship with God evolved—from formal and fearful to intimate and free.

How my pain began to make sense.
How my story, once heavy with shame, became fertile ground for purpose.
How healing led me home to myself.

If you've ever asked God for one thing and received something completely different—something you didn't recognize as a blessing at first—this is for you.

This isn't just a book.
It's a mirror to see yourself clearly,
A map to help you navigate the fog,
And a companion for anyone walking through loss, trauma, or survival.

Welcome to my story.
I hope it helps you rewrite yours.

SECTION ONE:

The Seed

Photo credit: Briana Cobb

CHAPTER 1

A Generational Curse

Nov 4, 2015

*I*t was fall, my favorite season—when the leaves shift into gold, crimson, and rust, and float gently to the ground, reminding us that everything beautiful must still come to an end. The air carried a crisp chill that sliced through the layers of clothes I had bundled on to stay warm. Beneath it all, my stomach still ached faintly from my C-section—an invisible scar from the life I had just brought into the world. I was holding so much: the changing weather, my tender body, and a soul stretched thin.

I stood facing the water—still, vast, and oddly familiar. It felt like it was calling to me, whispering promises of peace, asking only for one step forward.

I had walked this path many times before, reading gas meters for Consumers Energy. A year and six months into the job, I was preparing to be promoted to the service department, expecting a $3 raise from my $18-an-hour wage.

At 23, I was a young woman from the east side of Detroit. My new position required walking 8 to 10 miles a day. And I took it seriously. I felt lucky to be making that kind of money. So, I kept my head down, didn't ask questions nor build friendships. I wasn't there to connect—I was there to survive.

I was pregnant when I started the job but kept it hidden from my supervisor; afraid they wouldn't hire me if they knew. I worked straight through the pregnancy, barely slowing down. After the surgery, I took exactly eight weeks off—no more, no less—and came right back like nothing had happened. It wasn't strength. It was survival mode in its rawest form.

Behind those homes—neatly kept, peaceful, aspirational—was a lake I'd come to know well. I often got lost on my routes, but somehow, this spot always found me.

Here, I felt free.

But on this day, the water didn't just call to me—it pulled at me.

I was tired. Not just physically, but soul tired. The kind of tiredness that sleep can't touch. Years of silenced grief had calcified into numbness, but beneath it all, I was still tender. Still breaking.

I thought of the peace the water might bring—what it might feel like to surrender to it completely. Maybe then, I'd feel something. Maybe the weight would lift. Maybe I could stop pretending.

Then came a darker thought: My father died by suicide. A gunshot to the head. If he could do it . . . maybe this ache runs in the blood.

But the truth has a way of breaking through.

I remembered the murmurs—the way the family whispered that it never quite made sense. The two people who were there didn't call for help. The way he had seemed happy. How confusing it all still is.

And then—I thought of her.

My daughter.

In that instant, the ache inside me shifted. She wasn't just a reason to live, she was a mirror, a reminder that I was no longer living only for myself. The thought of her tiny hands, her breath rising and falling while she slept, snapped something back into place. I realized I couldn't teach her how to hold herself together if I gave in to falling apart. That moment made me a mother in a new way—aware, awake, and accountable.

A rustle in the trees pulled me out of the trance. I stepped back from the edge. I took out my phone and captured a photo of the lake—still, heavy, beautiful.

I didn't know it at the time, but that picture would become a marker. A turning point.

Not the end—

But the beginning of a return to myself.

CHAPTER 2

"Hold Your Ear"

Detroit, MI 1999

I learned early that beauty came with warnings.

"Hold your ear."

I sat on the stepping stool in my mama's kitchen while she sat behind me, pressing a hot comb through thick sections of my hair. The hiss of metal against the stove still lives in my body like a memory you don't speak but always feel. She'd test the heat with a paper towel, then glide the comb through my roots, chasing out every curl and kink like they were unwelcome.

The smell was unmistakable: a mix of singed hair and Blue Magic grease melting into my scalp. Thick and petroleum-based, that blue grease was the universal scent of Saturday afternoons in Black households—equal parts preparation and preservation. She'd part my hair with the tail of a rat-tooth comb, grease my scalp line by line, and press each section flat before the smoke even cleared. The ritual was painful and familiar, sacred and routine.

I'd press my index finger to my ear just like I was told, wondering every single time: "But what about my finger?" That part was never protected. It always struck me, even as a child. I was guarding myself from being burned by allowing myself to be burned. And somehow, that made sense to everyone.

It was one of my first lessons in self-sacrifice—how I learned to endure pain quietly if it meant keeping the peace or preserving an image. And I wasn't alone. This kind of silent suffering wasn't just personal—it was generational. Passed down like an heirloom in Black households where survival often meant shrinking, silencing, and enduring. We inherited the unspoken rules right along with the hot combs and hair grease.

※

My mama was 5'2", fair-skinned, with a wide, unforgettable smile and a signature gap she never tried to hide. She was soft-spoken and reserved, as if she was always thinking—always trying to figure things out before she spoke. She didn't raise her voice much, but there was something about her presence that still commanded respect. We were only sixteen years apart, but the closeness in age didn't bring us closer in connection. If anything, it felt like she stayed quiet to avoid saying the wrong thing. Whether it was discipline or guidance, she often chose silence over confrontation. She didn't offer affection in the ways I longed for—not in words or touch—but her care showed up in practical ways: making sure my hair was pressed, the bills were paid, and we had what we needed. In our world, that was the language of love.

Any time the comb slipped too close to the neck or ear, there'd be a quick yelp, then a phrase every Black girl knows like a chant: "Beauty is pain."

Pain became the price of presentation. But by then, the damage wasn't just physical.
It was emotional.
Cultural.
Spiritual

We had all internalized the idea that being **ourselves**—in our natural state—was never quite enough.

We were praised when we looked "done."
And to stay "done," we learned to avoid joy.

We couldn't sweat.
Couldn't swim.
Couldn't run around like the boys.
Couldn't get our edges wet or our hair "puffy."

So, I learned early how to shrink my fun and my freedom just to maintain an image.
Because hair that frizzed or curled up was seen as a problem.
Undone. Unacceptable.... Un...protected.

One day during a hair session, trying to make conversation, I told my mama something I thought would make her laugh.

> "Granny showed me how to roll one of those . . .
> blunts," I said, half-grinning, half-testing the words
> as they left my mouth—more curious than bold,
> unsure if it would land as funny or get me in trouble.

I was seven.
I didn't smoke. I just knew how.
And more than that, I just wanted **her** to respond. To see me.
To talk to me.

My mama was mostly quiet. I was the talker. I filled silence like
it was a void that needed my words to matter. But that day—
she went still.
Not angry. Just . . . tight.

I didn't understand the silence.
But I felt it.
It wrapped around me like shame I didn't have the words for yet.

Later that night, I heard arguing.
First between my mama and my dad.
Then my dad and his mother.

Voices raised. Blame flying. Tension cutting through the walls.

Soon after, my granny pulled me aside.

> "You weren't supposed to tell anyone that," she
> whispered, sharp but hushed.

And just like that, I became the problem.
The secret-keeper.
The reason people were upset.

No one explained.
No one asked me what I meant.
No one reassured me that I didn't do anything wrong.

And so, I blamed myself.
I carried the guilt.
I absorbed the confusion.

That moment taught me that speaking my truth—trying to connect—could hurt people.
Could cause conflict.
Could get me shushed.

So, I began to monitor my voice.
Filter my stories.
Pick and choose what was "safe" to share.

The irony is, all I ever wanted was closeness.

But I learned that connection came with rules I didn't understand.
Rules that made me shrink to fit inside them.

That longing to be seen, to connect, didn't disappear. It just buried itself under memories of better times—times that almost convinced me we were whole.

�֎

My dad was about 5'6". A darker shade of brown than my mother. Nice clean cut and always smelled good. Both of my parents were the oldest among their siblings, and my dad carried himself with the kind of confidence that made people feel safe.

He was a carefree spirit in many ways—always dressed in the latest fashions, always moving with ease. But he was also brilliant. A technical engineer for Ford, he knew how to take things apart and put them back together again—machines, bikes, stereos. Maybe even people, in the ways he tried to hold us all together.

He took pride in caring for his family. He loved to BBQ—standing in the backyard with his grill tongs like a king at his post, ribs sizzling, music playing, a towel slung over his shoulder like he was on stage. He wasn't just showing off; he was feeding us, protecting us, pouring into us.

He had a Corvette, an old school Cutlass, a Ford F-150 (which he swore he'd buy me when I turned 18), and a motorcycle he'd ride me on, my arms wrapped tight around his waist, the wind pulling at my cheeks as we weaved through side streets like nothing could touch us. He'd challenge my mama to race in his Corvette from my Nanna's house to ours—cutting through back roads just to see who'd make it home first. They laughed like they were still kids themselves, like they'd found a way to pause time.

He was present. He taught me and my younger brother how to ride bikes. My brother caught on quicker than I did, but I didn't mind. I was fine with my training wheels, content in the safety of what I knew.

It seemed like we had everything a family was supposed to have—stability, laughter, a sense of belonging. Especially because a two-parent married household was rare back then. People looked up to my parents. They often took in their younger siblings or cousins who needed a place to stay in our 3 bedroom bungalow.

But beneath the surface of what looked like peace were two young adults trying to outrun the shadows of their own childhoods. Both of their fathers had been absent. Their mothers, like so many Black women of that era, worked nonstop—holding entire households together on their own. Love often showed up as food on the table or clothes on your back, but not always as presence or guidance.

So my parents raised themselves, and then—without much of a blueprint—tried to raise us. They bought a home, got married, and did the best they could. But no one had shown them how to sit with discomfort, how to resolve conflict without shutting down or walking away. And the truth was, they hadn't learned how to repair what broke—inside of them or between them. Survival had taught them how to keep going, not how to go deeper.

And survival, though necessary, can become a kind of ceiling. It robs you of the energy to imagine beyond the next crisis, to create instead of just endure.

✺

When my parents divorced, I was around eight or nine.
Old enough to remember the tension.
Young enough to still believe that love was something you could earn if you just behaved right, stayed out of the way, or made yourself useful enough to keep.

My mama worked constantly after the separation. Not just to survive—but to *stay upright*. She had been diagnosed with Lupus well before I was born, and though I didn't understand what that meant, I knew that sometimes she was there, and sometimes she was in the hospital. And even when she was home, she often felt far away.

Some days, she'd move quietly through the house in her robe, bareheaded. Her hair never fully returned after chemo, and the scarring on her scalp made her sensitive in more ways than one. She wore wigs before they were stylish—before they were about trends or aesthetics—back when they were simply a form of covering. A way to preserve what illness tried to take.

I didn't know how to feel watching her like that. I'd look away sometimes, uncomfortable in ways I didn't know how to explain. Embarrassed, yes—but also guilty for being embarrassed. I felt sorry for her all the time, but I didn't have the language for it. Just a lump in my throat and a heart that didn't know where to put the ache.

Fatigue clung to her like weight in her bones.
Trying to recover. Trying to work. Trying to keep us afloat.
She was strong in ways I couldn't yet see—but as a child, I didn't interpret it that way.

I didn't see strength.
I saw distance.
I saw silence.
I felt invisible.

Before the divorce, my dad felt like home. Afterwards, he felt like a guest who didn't stay long enough to get comfortable. He popped in from time to time, but never with any real rhythm I could rely on. His presence was more like a breeze—welcomed when it came, but gone before I could ever hold onto it. When he did show up, it was usually to take my brother and me to my Granny's house on his side of the family.

Those visits were some of my fondest early memories. Her home was always full—of noise, of cousins, of laughter spilling out from the kitchen, of music drifting through the walls like a warm hum. My three aunts were always around, busy with their own children, but they made sure we never felt like outsiders just because our time with them was limited.

Even as a child, I carried a quiet resentment during those visits—an ache that settled in my chest when my dad wasn't there. I'd scan the room, hoping he'd walk through the door, and when he didn't, a small weight would press down on my joy. But the moment he did appear, it was like the sun came out just for me. My whole body would light up with excitement, and all was temporarily forgiven.

He would take us to Belle Isle, where the wind off the water makes everything feel wide and free.

Belle Isle is like a magical pocket tucked inside the city—an island park floating in the Detroit River, just between the U.S. and Canada. To a child, it felt like a whole other world. You have to drive across a bridge to get there, which made it feel like a secret destination, like we were leaving the city behind and entering something sacred.

The island is full of open green spaces and big shady trees that seemed to dance in the breeze. Families filled the picnic areas, music poured from car speakers, the smell of barbecue lingered in the air, and kids chased each other barefoot across the grass. There was a zoo back then, and a conservatory full of tropical plants that felt like stepping into a jungle. Water surrounding you on all sides—blue-gray and endless, with freighters slowly drifting by and the Canadian skyline across the way.

Belle Isle was where joy lived out loud. It was where I saw Black families gather, unwind, and celebrate life. For those few hours, it felt like everything was okay. Like I belonged.

We'd run across the grass and climb on the playground. I remember the giant slide that towered over me like a skyscraper. I was terrified of it. But Granny—who always smelled like cocoa butter and wrapped me in hugs that made the world feel small and safe—climbed up with me and slid down so I wouldn't have to face my fear alone.

That was the kind of love she offered—She wasn't what most people would call nurturing, but her love was raw and real. She was bold, protective, and deeply present when it mattered.

And then there were the dance circles. Music would blast from the speakers and the kids would take turns showing off their moves. I was too shy to join in, always hovering at the edge. But then my dad, in all his awkward charm, would step into the circle and pull me in with him. We'd dance offbeat and goofy, laughing the whole time. It was one of the rare times I felt seen by him—really seen. Like he wasn't just my dad, but someone who wanted to share joy with me, even if just for a moment.

Still, those visits were fleeting—bright bursts of joy and chaos that always ended too soon. And when the weekend faded and my dad disappeared again, I'd find myself floating between my Nanna's house and my Great Aunt's. My mother's mother and her mother's sister took turns looking after my younger brother and me.

At my Nanna's house, the energy slowed, and the silence was thicker.

Unlike the full, noisy rooms at my Granny's, Nanna's house carried a different kind of rhythm—quieter, steadier. She did her best to fill the hollow space left in the wake of my parents' absence—doing what she could to keep my hands busy and my mind engaged. In many ways, she succeeded.

She gave me little things to focus on: puzzles that challenged my patience, crochet hooks that kept my fingers looping yarn into soft, tangled shapes. We sat side by side working on paint-by-number kits, our heads bent low over the pages, the quiet hum of her presence soothing something restless in me. When we weren't inside, we were in the yard—her sanctuary that became mine too. I had full reign to explore every inch of it. For hours, I'd wander barefoot across the patchy grass and hardened dirt, refusing to wear shoes no matter how many times I stubbed my toes. I loved the way the earth felt beneath me—cool and spongy under the trees, dry and gritty in the sun.

There was a rusty swing on her wide porch, and I'd lay across it for what felt like forever, letting it rock gently as I stared up at the sky, getting lost in the movement of clouds. I made mud pies with leaves tucked in as garnish, dug holes so deep I was convinced I'd reach the earth's core—or maybe discover some long-lost treasure. Every time I found a smooth or oddly shaped rock, I added it to my growing collection, storing them in an old shoebox I kept under my bed like sacred artifacts.

I remember the sensation of hot concrete warming the soles of my feet, the rough bark of the trees I climbed scraping my palms, and the thrill of being eye-level with the birds for just a moment. And when I wasn't outside chasing magic, I had books—my first taste of freedom through imagination. They gave me places to go when my world felt too small.

Mystery stories like *Sherlock Holmes* gave my restless mind something to solve—at a time when the outside world felt like a puzzle I couldn't quite piece together.

I also loved *Junie B. Jones* and silly joke books—the kind that made me laugh out loud and feel like someone understood the way my brain worked.

Stories gave me a world where problems had solutions, endings made sense, and girls were chosen—where someone always came back for you. It gave me a sense of hope that maybe things could turn out okay, even if real life didn't feel that way yet.

In her own quiet, loving way, my Nanna helped me build a world of wonder, even in the midst of so much unknown.

But even with all the activities, all the busyness, I was absorbing quiet lessons about what love and belonging seemed to require. My parents' separation and their absence left me unanchored. Even though I was surrounded by family, I didn't feel securely held. I didn't know where I fit. So I watched, listened, and adjusted. I learned that love meant not needing too much. That being "good" and "easy" was the safest way to stay wanted.

I became hard on myself in small, silent ways. If I spilled something at someone's house, panic flared up inside me—afraid I'd seem messy or careless. If I accidentally broke something, I'd carry the guilt for days. I never wanted to be a problem. Or worse—a burden.

I even learned to pretend I wasn't hungry.
Even when my stomach growled, I'd say I was fine. I didn't want to be the kid who asked for too much or made anyone uncomfortable.

Better to stay small.
Better to stay out of the way.
Better to be wanted for my silence than rejected for my need.

No one ever said these things out loud. I don't believe it was anyone's intent to make me feel that way.
But it was the message I received.
And it stayed with me—long after the puzzles, the books, and the backyard adventures faded into memory.

❋

Writing this next part of the book has been one of the hardest things I've done. Even now, the memories sit heavy—difficult to access, harder to hold. There were days I stared at these pages, wondering if I should skip this part altogether. But I won't. Because this pain isn't just mine—it's shared by so many. So many people are walking around with grief they were never allowed to name.

And as painful as it's been to revisit, the writing has become healing.

Because the moment I gave my parents' stories space... I gave myself permission to grieve all the things I never let myself feel.

That's where healing begins.

CHAPTER 3

The Longest Day of the Year

(June 21, 2003 The Summer Solstice)

*I*n Detroit, summer evenings stretched endlessly. Kids played outside until the streetlights blinked on, the air thick with laughter, chalk dust, and the smell of someone grilling a few houses down.

I remember running around my great aunt's basement with my younger brother and older cousins.

"I bet you scared to jump from the top step to the bottom!" someone yelled.

We made up some of the best games back then.

Before phones, before tablets, before group chats and notifications—we had imagination and each other. We were the inventors of joy, turning sidewalks into storylines and backyards into battlegrounds. Our games had no rules, just dares and wild ideas. We'd challenge each other to leap over fences, run to the end of the block with our eyes closed, or ring a doorbell and dash before anyone answered.

We built obstacle courses from milk crates and old tires. Hide-and-seek became a neighborhood-wide mission. Tag felt like the Olympics.

We rode our bikes for hours—no gears, no helmets, just wind in our faces and scraped-up knees. We popped wheelies, rode three on one bike at a time—one on the back pegs, another on the handlebars—and dared each other to pedal without touching the grips. The sun watched us grow darker by the hour, our skin kissed bronze by joy.

Laughter echoed down the block like music. Somebody was always laughing—deep belly laughs, breathless giggles, that kind of joy that comes from knowing the world is still wide open and yours for the taking.

And when the streetlights flickered on, nobody had to call us. That warm amber glow was our signal: time to head to the porch. Time to wind down. But not to go in—not yet. We'd sit cross-legged with mosquito-bitten legs, swapping ghost stories or watching the older cousins flirt and dance to slow jams on somebody's speaker. Our mamas would yell from the windows when it got too late, but we soaked up every second we could.

That was the last summer I remember being completely free— before everything changed.

Before silence became a second skin.
Before I understood what it meant to hold pain in my body.

But in that moment, in that summer, we were just kids.
Wild, loud, fearless.

Free.

Everything seemed so big—especially the basement.
The air was damp and warm, the carpet old and hard beneath
our bare feet. Light filtered in from the tiny ground-level
windows, just enough to let our imaginations run wild.

Then I heard it.

My mama screamed from upstairs: "NO! NO! NO!"

Everyone froze. Panic sliced through the air.
We all ran up the stairs to the second floor, hearts pounding.
The den was filled with a strange stillness. My mama stood
alone, holding the phone to her ear, frozen in shock.

"What's wrong, Ma?" I asked, already feeling the panic rise in
my chest.

She didn't answer. Her face was blank with horror, her body
trembling. She sobbed, and it was as if my heart already knew
what my ears hadn't yet heard. I felt something in me break.

Then she ran.

She rushed up the stairs toward the third floor, where my great aunt was. Her movements were frantic, grief-stricken. I watched her struggle to carry herself up each step.

We sat silently on the green shag carpet that lined the stairs, listening, trying to make sense of what had just happened. The house cat darted between us as our ears strained for any piece of information. My cousins and I whispered guesses, each of us grasping for understanding in a moment that defied it.

Then my older cousin looked at me, his face pale. "They said Boo died."

"My dad?" I asked, my voice shaking.

My palms began to sweat. My stomach twisted. The spaghetti from dinner threatened to come up.

Dads don't die . . . right?
My mind tried to make it make sense.

I had known dads to leave. To come and go.
Some kids never knew their fathers.
But no one I knew had ever had their mom get a call saying:

"Boo is dead. He shot himself."

Everyone began to cry, so I cried too. But inside, I felt nothing. I forced out a cry because it felt like what I was supposed to do.

Emotionally, my system shut down. My survival mode clicked on. I cried so hard I began to shake and vomit. My cousins wrapped their arms around me, trying to comfort me. I shook them off and ran to the shaggy green carpet and laid on the floor in front of the couch, pressing my cheek into its plush familiarity.

The scent of carpet powder and the vacuum offered a strange kind of comfort. Something familiar in the chaos. Something grounding.

I wouldn't allow myself to believe it was happening.

People began to arrive as each hour ticked away. The air thickened with grief. Every new voice carried a new layer of pain:

" . . . doesn't make sense."
" . . . not like him to kill himself."
" . . . two people with him."
" . . . why didn't his girlfriend and her brother call for help?"
" . . . cops ruled it a suicide. Case closed."

I sobbed myself to sleep, hoping I would wake up and none of it would be real.

Grief doesn't follow a straight line. It doesn't ask for permission, and it certainly doesn't wait until you're ready. In the days between my father's death and his funeral, time felt both frozen and frantic. One moment I was staring at the wall in a fog, the next I was helping pick out clothes for the service like any of it made sense.

The world kept spinning—cars passed, TV shows aired, the sun still rose—but inside, everything had gone silent.
I remember walking down the hall and pausing at the mirror, half-expecting to see someone else's face. Someone older.
Someone who knew how to handle this kind of pain.
But I didn't. I saw me—ten years old, scared, trying to look normal when nothing felt normal anymore.

And yet, life filled the space between tragedy.
There were awkward conversations, meals from neighbors, phone calls with long pauses.
There were moments of laughter that slipped out too soon, followed by guilt.
Grief is strange that way—it doesn't erase the ordinary; it just makes it heavier.
Every sound, every smell, every question carried new meaning.

The way my body flinched at sudden noises, the tightness in my chest I couldn't name, the way I held my breath in unfamiliar places—it all began here, long before I had the language for anxiety or trauma.

I didn't know it then, but those in-between days were the beginning of something I'd spend years trying to name: the long, complicated becoming of someone who had survived the unthinkable.

Two weeks later, we arrived at the funeral home.
The smell hit me first—wilting flowers, strong perfume, and

something cold and sterile.

The room was too quiet. Not peaceful quiet—**wrong** quiet. Like the walls were holding their breath.
Relatives whispered in hushed tones, their voices a low hum. I didn't want to look at anyone.

But then I saw it.

The casket. Bright white, polished, too real. It gleamed under the lights like something out of place.

He was there. My dad.

Just a few weeks ago, he was alive. Holding my hand as we walked downtown Detroit, reminding my brother and me not to split the pole.

And now . . . this.
Inside that box.
Anger gripped me.

Even though he had taken a gunshot to the head, the family chose an open casket.

I screamed. My chest tightened. My knees gave out.

My dad's middle sister grabbed me and pulled me into the hallway. I wanted to leave. Everything felt wrong.

Eventually, I was led back in.

He didn't look like himself. His skin was pale, his face swollen, his lips tinted unnaturally.

The coolest man I knew, gone.

The guy whose off-rhythm dance moves, laugh, and perfectly aligned smile could light up any room and break people out of their shells.
The man who would empty starch cans for the perfect crease in his pants.
Who taught me to always put my socks on before my pants.
Who had promised to give me the world . . .
Was reduced to a still, waxy shell.

Someone nearby was crying. The sound irritated me.
My gut twisted, not just with grief—but with fear.

Because if my dad could vanish like that, what else could be taken from me?

I didn't have an answer. I only knew nothing felt safe anymore.

The preacher began:
"Dear brothers and sisters, today we gather in grief, in sorrow, and in love . . . "

I barely registered the words.

But my great-grandmother (on my mama's side) did.

She sat beside me in the front row, her Bible clasped tight in her brown, wrinkled hands.

Every time the preacher mentioned God, she rolled her eyes.

When he shouted, "But God!" she shouted right back, "Which one?!"

My heart pounded. I looked around—was anyone else hearing this?

I was embarrassed. I thought she might get thrown out.

I feared both sides of my family would start fighting.

Whose side would I take?

But no one said a word to her.
She was our matriarch.
She was small, but no one dared challenge her.
I remembered it always being that way.

Even at my young age, I understood that her anger wasn't just about my father's death.

She didn't like that this man worshipped a different God than hers.

Filled with confusion, I couldn't help but admire her courage.
Her conviction.

That stuck with me, shaped me in ways I wouldn't understand
until years later.

Still, I wanted her to be quiet.
I wanted the noise to stop.
I wanted the confusion to stop.

After the funeral, I didn't go to the burial.
I still haven't, to this very day.

Time moved forward. But nothing felt normal.

The nights were the worst.
The sun gave me cover. I could pretend. I could hide.
But night left me exposed.
My sleepless nights began.

✳

My Hello Kitty clock blinked: **1:26 AM.**

My chest rose and fell with shallow breaths. Every creak in the
house made my heart race.

My room, once soft and pink, felt like a cage.
The ceiling felt heavy, like it knew my secret:
I was scared. More scared than I'd ever been.

Then the nightmares came.

I'd be barefoot in the backyard. Pajamas soaked in wet grass.
The trees too still.
My dad would be standing far away—crooked, silent.

His eyes were wrong. Too wide. Too hollow.

His mouth opened, trying to speak, but no sound came.

I'd scream—but my voice wouldn't work.
I'd try to run, but the ground held my feet.

He'd whisper, **"Why didn't you save me?"** in a voice that didn't sound like his.

I'd wake up gasping, drenched in sweat, my sheets twisted like ropes.

I couldn't go back to sleep.

So, I'd pop in a VHS.
The *Lion King* was my favorite.

But when the tape ended, the silence returned.
So did the question:

Why did he leave me?

That question held everything: fear, abandonment, loneliness. It clung to me like a second skin.

Maybe I wasn't enough to stay for.
Maybe I was never enough.

Morning would come.
The alarm would ring.

Time to pretend again.

More silence.
More looking into my mother's hollow eyes and knowing—we were both haunted.

Just by different ghosts.

Rooted Reflections: Your Turn

**These worksheets after each section are for anyone who has ever questioned their worth, carried unspoken grief, or shaped themselves to survive. Let this be your space to pause, name what's been buried, and begin the gentle process of returning to yourself.

Section One: The Seed

Scripture: John 12:24
"Very truly I tell you, unless a kernel of wheat falls to the ground and dies, it remains only a single seed. But if it dies, it produces many seeds."

Spiritual Insight:

This section begins in the dark — the kind of darkness that makes you question if you'll ever see light again. But in the spiritual world, the dark is not the end. It's where all sacred things begin; in the soil, in the silence, in the secret wrestling of the soul. Your choice to live was a seed — planted in defiance of the pain that tried to bury you. That moment was more than survival. It was the breaking of a generational curse. The beginning of new roots.

· What "seed moment" in my life felt like death, but actually began my transformation?
· What generational pattern am I being called to break?
· How can I honor what I've buried without carrying the weight of it anymore?

If you felt something stir in you while reflecting, the prompts below are designed to help you go deeper — into memory, into grief, into growth.

1. Memory Mapping

Think back to a time in your childhood when you felt that you were expected to be strong, quiet, or "good."

- What was happening around you?
- What message did you receive (spoken or unspoken) about your needs or emotions?
- How do you think that memory shaped how you show up today?

✐ *Write or sketch your response below:*

_____

_____

_____

_____

_____

2. Survival Mode Signals

When you're in survival mode, you may notice yourself doing things like:

- Numbing or avoiding emotions
- Silencing your needs
- Over-giving to feel safe
- Shrinking to avoid rejection

Which of these patterns feel familiar to you? What do you think they were trying to protect you from?

✐ *Reflect and list below:*

_____

_____

_____

_____

_____

3. Grief That Was Never Named

Grief doesn't only come from death. Sometimes it's the loss of safety, innocence, connection, or being truly seen.
· Is there grief you've carried silently?
· What would it look like to give that grief a voice now?

✐ *Allow yourself to write without judgment:*

_____

_____

_____

_____

_____

4. A Seed You're Ready to Plant

What truth are you now ready to name?
What part of you are you reclaiming, even if it's just a whisper?

✐ *Let this be your beginning:*

_____

_____

_____

_____

_____

Take your time. Come back to this as many times as you need.
You are not broken. You are becoming.

SECTION TWO:

Taking Root

CHAPTER 4

The "Straight" and Narrow Path

*F*rom my preteen years into young adulthood, I began to quietly unravel.

The moments I once shared with my mama—hot combs hissing on the stove, her gentle hands pressing out my curls—were replaced by chemical relaxers. Creamy, stinging potions that promised straight hair in exchange for scalp burns. I'd sit still, teeth clenched, trying to time the rinse just right to avoid scabs. No one warned us about the long-term damage. We just knew that straight meant beautiful. Straight meant "kept." Straight meant acceptable.

But behind the sleek hair was a girl learning to survive in silence.

My mother and I were already drifting apart long before the distance became visible. After the death of my dad, grief swallowed her whole—but life didn't pause. Bills still came. I watched her try to hold everything together: enrolling in school to finish her degree, climbing the ranks at work to become a manager, balancing more than most people could imagine.

By eighth grade, I had already attended several middle schools. Each move came from necessity, not choice—my mama's tireless attempts to find stability beneath our feet. But the constant uprooting made it harder to find my own. Every new school meant new faces, new discomfort, and no time to process the grief and trauma still echoing through our family.

Her illness only deepened the weight. Doctor visits, flare-ups, and sleepless nights replaced her plans. Eventually, we had to move back in with my Nanna—our version of starting over.

When I wasn't at Nanna's, I'd walk down the street to my great-aunt's house. My mother's side of the family lived close—porches within steps, Sunday dinners always just a phone call away. My great-grandmother had seven children—five daughters and two sons—and raised them to stay close, to protect one another at all costs. Unity was her legacy. But she was also raising them in faith.

When Jehovah's Witnesses knocked on her door, she was moved by the message—a promise of hope and purpose. It became her mission to pass that truth down to her children, to offer something more than survival.

By the time I was born, the religion was already stitched into our family's rhythm—woven into conversations, decisions, and expectations—even if I didn't fully understand what it meant.

In the early years, that closeness felt like a safety net. We were a web of cousins and aunties who felt like second mothers. But as the family tree stretched—more children, more opinions, more distance—something began to fray.

We inherited survival, yes. But the tools to navigate one another's differences? The space to ask for help, speak our truths, or simply be seen? That part never made it down the line.

I often wondered why no one noticed I was quietly unraveling.

I didn't really know how to take care of myself. I was the oldest child, the big sister. And coming from a line of strong Black women—who I was often reminded had endured far worse than I had—I was expected to just know and to figure it out. To toughen up. To be strong.

So I learned to lean on myself.

Not because I was ready, but because no one was coming to show me how. So I started teaching myself.

I'd spend hours in my great aunt's bathroom, scarf in hand, watching the mirror as I twisted and tied and wrapped my hair until it finally looked right—until *I* finally looked right. The sink was old but spotless, porcelain chipped just enough to show its age. The overhead light buzzed faintly, casting a yellow hue that made my skin look sallow, but I didn't care—I was determined to fix myself.

Behind me stood the built-in cabinets, short and narrow with latches that clicked like secrets. I used to climb inside them during hide and seek, curling my knees to my chest, holding my breath so no one would hear me giggling behind the door. They used to feel like a castle. Now they felt too small, too childish—a silent reminder that I had outgrown the spaces that once made me feel safe. It was time to grow up.

I had cried out for help with my hair, only to be met with laughter from my older cousins—left to figure it out on my own, just like so many other things still to come. But I was determined to not become undone. My scarf was my armor, my mirror the only witness to my becoming. I pulled and smoothed and adjusted, trying to mold myself into something acceptable, something presentable, something worthy of being seen. The bathroom, with its blue and white tiled floor and faint scent of Avon powder, had become my makeshift sanctuary and battlefield—where I faced my reflection and wrestled with who I was allowed to be.

I watched cousins my age being cared for by their older sisters. They wore matching outfits—Air Force 1s, the latest Jordans. Meanwhile, I rotated through hand-me-downs from my mother's closet, slipping into her shoes once our sizes matched. I didn't keep up with the latest trends, but people assumed I had it all— because of how my life had started.

I had a dad.

I had the oldest of the seven sisters as my grandmother.

My Nanna—who prioritized me, poured into me, made me feel seen in ways others didn't. But even that came at a cost. Nanna was stretched thin trying to be everything to everyone—her children, her grandchildren, her sisters and brothers and their children. I was made to feel guilty for being loved.

They said I was favored. That I was spoiled. That I was too sensitive.

And so, I became an outsider. Left out of trips. Left out of inside jokes.

Unsupported. Misunderstood.

✳

It was around that time that I consciously reached for the religion that was woven into my upbringing, made it my own, and tried to believe with all my heart.

At first, it felt like structure.

I reached for comfort wherever I could find it—somewhere with rules, somewhere with answers, somewhere I could feel . . . chosen.

I decided to dedicate my life to being a Jehovah's Witness. And for a while, it felt like safety.

I wasn't obligated to attend the Kingdom Hall. My great-aunt required her children to go, but since I was a guest in her home, I had more of a choice. Still, we were expected to participate in the Watchtower study—reading and highlighting the articles in preparation to answer questions during meetings on Sundays and Wednesdays. These weren't just ordinary readings; they were structured, guided lessons designed to teach us how to interpret the Bible the way the organization saw fit. The articles walked us through scriptures with pre-framed explanations, and we were encouraged to underline specific lines and rehearse answers that aligned with the teachings.

It was framed as spiritual preparation, a way to "rightly divide the word of truth." But over time, it felt less like learning the Bible and more like learning how to recite what we were told the Bible meant. The format left little room for curiosity or personal reflection—only reinforcement. Participation wasn't just expected, it was a measure of your spiritual standing. If you didn't comment, people noticed. If you missed too many studies, questions were asked.

For a child craving validation, it was both comforting and quietly pressurizing—to be seen for answering correctly, but never quite feeling free to explore what I personally believed or wondered.

We'd all study together around the dining room table, and I

loved it. I felt included. Cared for. When I first started attending meetings, people would smile warmly, welcoming me in. I was praised for raising my hand and answering questions I had studied for. And when you gave your first public comment, the congregation clapped—a small but powerful form of acknowledgment I had been craving.

So, I poured in more.

As I got older, I wanted more opportunities to prove my worth. I aspired to be promoted to auxiliary pioneer—a title given to those who volunteered a set number of hours each month to preaching and door-to-door ministry. It wasn't a paid role, but in the eyes of the congregation, it was a badge of honor. It meant you were serious about your faith, willing to sacrifice your time for Jehovah, and on the path to deeper spiritual commitment. I wanted to be the best at whatever they offered—even if I didn't fully understand what I was signing up for or what it would cost me.

The elders suggested I begin studying one-on-one with a sister in the congregation. I agreed, and I quickly caught on. I had all the right answers.

Ironically, as my knowledge grew, so did my depression.

I was reading the scriptures, following every rule, doing all the right things. But none of it seemed to reach my heart. When I tried to talk about the sadness I was feeling, I was met with well-meaning—but shallow—verses:

"Do not be anxious about anything . . . "

(Philippians 4:6–7)

"Jehovah is close to the brokenhearted . . . "

(Psalm 34:18)

I read them. I recited them. But I was still sad. Still disconnected.

I didn't want to be seen as an unbeliever, or as spiritually weak, so I pretended to feel better. I internalized the idea that something had to be wrong with me if all this "truth" wasn't working.

Among my aunts and cousins, there were varying levels of belief— some devout, some indifferent. I lived in the tension between them. The rules were rigid. The expectations, suffocating.

"You shouldn't watch that movie."
"That music is inappropriate."
"Nothing comes before Jehovah—not even your family."

The growing sense of isolation only intensified.

We were taught, over and over again, not to associate with anyone who wasn't a Jehovah's Witness—including family. It wasn't always said outright, but scriptures like *1 Corinthians 15:33*, "Bad associations spoil useful habits," were quoted like warnings. The message was clear: stay inside the lines.

I tried making friends within the congregation, but even there, I felt like an outsider. I was labeled a "bad associate" more than once.

At gatherings, which were supposed to be youth fellowships, the adults would ask, *"Who are your parents?"* Their tone wasn't just curious—it was assessing. As if my worth depended on whether I came from a two-parent household, or if my family name held weight in the congregation.

Kids whose parents held titles—elders, pioneers—or had long-standing roots in the congregation were seen as more spiritually "stable." More acceptable.

※

Field service became both my proving ground and my punishment. I convinced myself that if I just tried harder—knocked on enough doors, spoke with enough conviction, logged enough hours—maybe I could become the kind of girl God would be proud of. Maybe someone would finally say, *"She's doing it right."*

The sun wasn't even high yet, but the Kingdom Hall parking lot was already filling with cars. Men in button-down shirts and slacks stood in small clusters, checking their watches and flipping through not-at-home lists. Women adjusted their skirts, smoothed their children's hair, and exchanged greetings that felt warm on the surface but rehearsed underneath.

I stood near the back of the group, quietly hoping to blend in, silently bracing for the tension I knew would come.

Field service always started the same—a short prayer, a territory map, and the shuffle of partner assignments. I used to dread the moment someone would suggest I go first. My palms would sweat as I knocked, Bible and magazine in hand, hoping no one would answer. If they did, I'd flash my best polite smile and try to remember the scripted lines, praying I wouldn't mess up.

No matter how many hours I logged, how early I showed up, or how neatly I dressed, it always felt like I was being watched—not with care, but with evaluation.

The seasoned pioneers never said it outright, but their smiles were tight. Their feedback felt more like correction than compassion:

> "Next time, let the householder respond before
> moving into the scripture."
> "Try offering the magazines with more confidence."
> "Only 8 hours this month?"

My dedication, my mindset, my loyalty—they were always being measured. Not publicly, but through side glances and subtle reminders. A scripture quoted at the end of a conversation. A raised brow. A lingering silence.

I tiptoed constantly—around words, expectations, even the way I carried myself. But even invisibility wasn't safe.

I still wasn't enough.

I was lonely. Desperate to be seen. Desperate to be enough.

I tried so hard to follow the rules. To be faithful. To be good. But no matter what I did, I couldn't win. Obedience made me invisible. Mistakes made me the center of shame.

God began to feel like a father I could never please—constantly testing me, waiting for me to fall short, setting me up to fail.

And yet—something in me stayed.

Because even inside that pressure cooker of perfectionism, there was structure. Purpose. Rhythm. And in the quiet moments between judgment and silence, I was learning.

I learned how to study, how to speak, and how to hold space with strangers. I learned presence.

Those public talks that made my knees shake? They became my first lessons in pacing and delivery. The door-to-door presentations? My first taste of writing, rewriting, and connecting. Even the rehearsed Watchtower reviews taught me how to extract meaning from text—something I still do today, but with freer hands.

In a strange way, field service kept me focused—and distracted. Much like my Nanna had once done with her busy hands and long to-do lists, the religion gave me something to organize. Something to measure. Something that made me feel like I was trying.

To the outside world, we were just well-dressed strangers on porches.

But for me, field service was both my stage and my shield. A place where I developed survival skills—even as it shrank the parts of me that longed to bloom.

Still, I held on. I believed if I just endured long enough, if I kept trying, there would be a breakthrough. A blessing. A revelation to make all of this make sense.

But it never came.

Instead, the sadness deepened and that sadness over time became anger and tension.
My reactions became sharp, explosive, desperate attempts to be heard or understood.

One day, we were all sitting on my Nanna's bed—me, her, and one of my older cousins. Something old was playing softly on the TV in the background, some classic movie or rerun she always kept on for comfort. I remember the flicker of the screen more than what was on it.

I don't remember what sparked the conversation, but I remember the sting when my cousin turned to me, frustration on her face, and asked, "What is wrong with you? Why are you always so angry?"

Her voice wasn't curious—it was annoyed.

I snapped. I wasn't yelling just to be heard—I was unraveling. I tried to explain the anger I carried, the ache of growing up without my mother consistently around.

"She's working," my cousin shrugged, dismissive. "She's just trying to live her life. None of our mamas were around like that."

My Nanna jumped in, as she always did when it came to my mama. Her voice was soft, her tone rehearsed. "You have to understand she's doing the best she can."

But I was already crying, the kind of crying that burns and trembles. "I just want my mama," I choked out.

And in that moment—no one moved. No one embraced me. No one saw my pain.

I felt invisible, like I was shouting into the wind.

For years after that, I couldn't understand why they couldn't hear me, why no one acknowledged what I was carrying. So I turned inward. I started to believe maybe I was the problem. Maybe I was too sensitive, too dramatic, too much.

I began to hate my emotions. I hated how deeply I felt things, especially when I was constantly reminded it was too deep. So I started praying to God—not for strength, not for peace, but for numbness.

"Take my feelings away," I begged.

And when they didn't go, I turned that pain into hatred.

Hatred for my emotions.

Hatred for my mother.

Hatred for myself.

Hatred for the life I had never asked for.

As time went on, I kept internalizing.

But no one saw.

Instead, what caught their attention was sex.

※

Like many young people craving connection, I sought comfort where I could find it.

What began as a relationship with someone I cared about eventually ended, and in time, I began seeing someone else. I was exploring intimacy, attachment, and what it meant to be wanted.

But in the eyes of the congregation, there was no space for complexity—only black and white. Right and wrong.

When rumors started spreading, I was summoned to meet with a judicial committee.

Four grown men sat across from me in a stuffy back room.

They opened with prayer, then asked me to recount every detail of my "immorality."

The room was small and still, but the constant clicking of a pen cut through the silence like a metronome of judgment—click, click, click—as they scribbled notes while I confessed the details of my so-called wrongdoing. One wall was lined with books— Bibles, encyclopedias, and dictionaries used for study and instruction. I stared at them in between the awkward silences, reading the titles just to avoid meeting their eyes. My long skirt clung to my legs, suddenly too hot and itchy. My throat felt dry, each word harder to push out than the last. My eyes burned, not just from holding back tears, but from the shame that wrapped itself around me like smoke.

It wasn't a conversation.
It was an interrogation—one cloaked in spiritual concern.

They wanted to know everything under the guise of helping me "repent."

But their job wasn't to understand.
It was to assess.
To determine whether I was still "worthy" of remaining in the congregation.

When they finished, they excused me to the hallway. Minutes later, I was called back—faced with stern expressions and rehearsed solemnity.

I was to be disfellowshipped.

After it was announced publicly, people I had grown up with passed me like I was invisible.

I felt numb—like I had swallowed the verdict before they even spoke it. Somewhere deep inside, I believed I deserved it. The humiliation settled into my chest, crushing my self-esteem beneath the weight of their stares and silence. I still attended meetings, unsure what else to do—but each time, I sat in silence, a ghost among the living.

�֎

It wasn't until years later that I found out others who had done far more—elders' children and grandchildren caught in patterns of open rebellion—had been quietly shielded. Protected.

Given second and third chances I never received.

As an adult and a mother, that realization shook me.
I began to see just how much control had been disguised as concern.
How often love was conditional—dependent on obedience, compliance, and appearance.
And how deeply the shame embedded in those years had followed me into womanhood.

✳

For Jehovah's Witnesses, the annual convention was supposed to be a spiritual highlight—a sacred gathering of hundreds, sometimes thousands, all united by one common theme. Believers from different congregations, cities, even states, filed into massive stadiums dressed in their best, smiling, hugging, exchanging warm greetings like a big family reunion in the name of God.

As we approached the convention hall, the summer heat shimmered off the pavement. My heels clicked against the sidewalk in rhythm with the crowd—families in their best, walking with purpose, Watchtower literature tucked neatly under arms. The building loomed ahead like a promise: air-conditioned, orderly, sacred.

But before we could cross the street, I heard him.

A man stood on the corner across from the entrance, gripping a microphone in one hand and a large handmade sign in the other. His voice cracked through the amplifier, urgent and sharp: "Turn away! Open your eyes! You're being deceived!"

His words cut through the steady hum of conversation and quickened footsteps. A few heads turned. Most didn't.

I slowed, confused, the sound of his voice tugging at something inside me. He didn't look angry—just desperate, like someone trying to warn a loved one before it's too late.

Then I heard my older cousin, just a few steps ahead, mutter under his breath to his sister,
"He's an apostate. He left the truth—and the Bible says they're worse than someone who never believed."

My heart thudded.

Apostate.
Worse than an unbeliever.

The words curled around my ribs like cold fingers.

I looked away from the man. I tightened my grip on my bag. I blocked out everything he was saying—not because it didn't make sense, but because I was terrified it might. Terrified that listening would pull me further off course, further away from the only place I had ever been taught to call safe.

So I turned my head, stepped forward, and tried to swallow the strange ache that had begun to form in my chest.

I tried to return to the flicker of happiness from that morning. It had been so long since I'd felt like I belonged anywhere, and the energy in the air was contagious—hopeful, reverent, charged. I had carefully prepared my outfit, arrived early, and tried to quiet the voice in my head that warned me not to expect too much.

But as I moved through the crowd, something became painfully clear.

No one was looking at me.
No one was smiling in my direction.
No one acknowledged me at all.

It was like I was invisible.

Hundreds of familiar faces—people I had once studied the Bible with, shared field service with, prayed beside—now passed me like I was a stranger. Some even looked past me deliberately, their gazes avoiding mine with practiced ease.

It was as if word had spread—fast and wide—that I was no longer clean. No longer worthy. That I had done something unforgivable, and the mere sight of me might contaminate their righteousness.

That was the thing about this kind of spiritual punishment—it didn't require a formal announcement. Just a quiet consensus.

A collective decision to pretend you no longer existed. To treat you like a cautionary tale, while never daring to ask how you got here in the first place.

I looked around the convention hall—at the sea of suits and modest dresses, the synchronized flipping of Bible pages, the orchestrated applause after each talk. The stage was perfectly lit. The banners were crisp. The program was flowing right on schedule.

But inside, I was crumbling.

The only thing tethering me to any sense of comfort was her—my mama. Ironically, during that season of being shunned, my mama and I grew closer.
It was one of the few times I felt her reach for me, not to punish, but to pull me back in.

I believe she truly thought she was helping—reconnecting me to what she believed was the truth.

And for a little while, it almost worked. In that moment, her presence mattered more than the silence of the crowd. At home, we had been growing closer. We laughed more. We watched movies together. Shared quiet moments reading the bible together that felt like tiny stitches repairing something frayed between us. For a while, it felt like we were finding our way back to each other. But at the convention, that closeness vanished. She sat beside me, smiling faintly, holding her Bible open, listening to the speaker with a look of calm conviction.

She didn't acknowledge the way people moved around us like we were an inconvenience. Or maybe she did and chose not to.

I didn't understand how it had come to this—how quickly a community could become an exile, how faith could be used like a weapon of shame.

I came hoping for renewal. Instead, I was reminded just how far outside the circle I'd already drifted.

But I had her.
Finally, she saw me.

For a moment, I thought things were starting to shift. My spirit felt just a little lighter—like if I could just keep showing up, keep praying, keep proving myself by abstaining from sex, maybe I could work my way back into favor. Maybe things would finally turn around.

I was doing everything I had been taught—attending meetings, studying, dressing modestly, smiling when it hurt. If I could just meet every expectation, maybe I could earn my place again.

Maybe I could be enough.

But I soon realized the warmth I had started to feel in our home was replaced by her practiced stillness—her loyalty, not to me, but to the obedience the religion demanded.

We were walking side by side at the convention center when I barely noticed her increasing her speed to put a slight distance between us. I quickened my pace to whisper something small, something ordinary—I had recognized someone from one of my classes and wanted to share the moment with her.

She shushed me quickly, sharply. Not with anger, but with something colder—quiet, practiced disapproval. Like my voice itself was offensive. Then, without a word, she waved me away and walked off, her expression unreadable.

And just like that, something inside me broke.

Whatever small bridge we had been trying to rebuild cracked beneath the weight of her silence. I felt myself withdraw—not in defiance, but in defeat. I pulled back even further into myself, where it was safer, where there were no expectations to fail.

Later, I would come to understand that her reaction wasn't entirely her own. It was part of the teaching. A form of "spiritual discipline" cloaked in the language of love. Jehovah's Witnesses were taught that when a child strays from the faith, silence is an act of obedience. Distance is supposed to stir repentance. Even a parent's love becomes conditional—weaponized as a tool to bring the "lost one" back.

They called it tough love.

But it felt like abandonment.

When I was finally accepted back into the congregation, I wasn't the same. I was colder. Guarded. Not just with her—but with everyone. I no longer trusted easily. I had learned that love here could vanish without warning, that acceptance came with terms, and silence came wrapped in spiritual justification.

No one helped me process it.
No one guided me gently back.
I was just expected to fall in line. Smile. Be grateful. Pretend like none of it ever happened.

But something had shifted. And I knew, deep down, I would never be the same.

Still, I maintained my image . . .
An image I wasn't even sure I believed in.
Still, I wrapped my hair each night.
Still showed up "put together."
Still wore the right clothes, sat in the right seats, and smiled the right smile.

And deep inside, I waited.
Waited for the reward I had been promised.
Waited for the peace I was told obedience would bring.
Waited for life to start feeling like it meant something.

But it never came.

This went on for years.

※

I barely graduated high school.

Not because I wasn't capable—but because by that time, my depression and anger had begun to seep out in immature, self-sabotaging ways. Looking back, I realize now that a lot of it was a cry for attention—a silent protest against years of being overlooked.

I had once been a 4.2 GPA student, thriving in academics, just months away from walking across the stage in honor cords and potential. But no one in my chaotic circle ever said, "Great job!" or "You're brilliant—what's next?" No one asked about my dreams or my future. The only question that ever came up was:

"How will you use your life to serve Jehovah?"

By then, it had already become painfully clear: I wasn't going to be one of the "chosen ones." Not the youth invited to speak at conventions. Not the girl celebrated from the platform with public praise.

No matter how many hours I poured into ministry, how flawless my answers were during study, or how confident I became at presentations—it was never enough. The recognition I quietly hoped for always seemed to pass over me, landing instead on others.

And I felt guilty for even noticing.
Guilty for wanting to be seen.

I convinced myself that craving acknowledgment meant I was being prideful. That I wasn't spiritual enough. That wanting to be valued made me selfish.

So I swallowed it—like I did everything else.

※

I remember overhearing one of my Nanna's friends ask if they'd be encouraging me to travel for college, maybe explore one of the scholarships I'd earned. The answer came quickly, almost scoffed out:

"Oh no, that's too dangerous."
"She needs to stay focused on Jehovah."
"There's no real value in secular education anyway."

These fear-drenched declarations were confusing. These were the people I trusted to guide me—and yet, every time an opportunity presented itself, they responded with warnings and restrictions.

When my school counselors tried to help me see the gravity of the opportunities I had—a full ride to Harvard or practically any school of my choice—I nodded politely but tuned them out. Their words sounded far away, muted by the voice in my head that had been shaped by years of religious conditioning:

Anything outside of Jehovah is a trap.
Anything that seems too good must be from Satan the Devil.

So, I shut it all down.

In the middle of the confusion, the noise, and my own inner war, I made a drastic decision. Months before graduation, I dropped out.

Just . . . stopped showing up. And the most heartbreaking part? No one I looked to for guidance tried to stop me.

Only one cousin pulled me aside one day and tried to talk some sense into me. She reminded me gently, but firmly,

"You don't have a father to fall back on. You don't have anyone to provide for you. What are you going to do financially?"

I looked her in the eye and said, with a blank kind of hope, "Jehovah will make a way."

I barely believed it as I said it.

Eventually, I enrolled in an alternative school and earned my high school diploma. Quietly.

No prom.

No celebration.

No big party.

Just a printed certificate . . . and the next day came like any other. Life didn't pause to applaud.

※

I wouldn't come to understand until much later that the choices I kept surrendering, the joy I kept silencing, and the dreams I kept setting aside were all fragments of the same quiet question:

Do I have the right to take up space as I am?

At the time, I didn't know how to answer that. So instead, I split myself in two.

There was the version of me that showed up at meetings, dressed modestly, reciting scriptures, trying to be everything the congregation expected. And then there was the other version— curious, restless, aching to be free.

She showed up on weekends, with family and friends who weren't Witnesses, in places I wasn't supposed to be, doing things I wasn't supposed to do.

It didn't feel like rebellion. It felt like relief.

But the weight of carrying both identities eventually took its toll.

And one night—a blur of craving connection, needing to feel seen—shifted everything.
The kind of night that leaves a mark you can't erase.

That's how I found myself pregnant.
By someone who wasn't a Jehovah's Witness.
And nothing in my life would ever be the same again.

CHAPTER 5

Something to Hold On To

I had perfected the art of living a double life.

It wasn't something I set out to do—it just . . . happened. Gradually. Quietly. Out of necessity.

Survival required shapeshifting. I learned to mirror whoever I was around. With one crowd, I could speak scripture fluently, quoting chapter and verse with practiced ease. With another, I could laugh too loud, drink too much, and dance away the ache in my chest like it wasn't even there.

On weekends, I'd be out with my older cousins—nights that blurred together, fueled by liquor and loud music. We drank until the world spun, until the pain dulled, until we were too far gone to remember what we were trying to forget.

Then Sunday would come, and I'd sit in the Kingdom Hall, clean and composed, physically present but spiritually checked out. Nodding in rhythm with the congregation, but inside, I was far away—numb, divided, pretending I still belonged.

I was only twenty-one but felt like an adolescent trapped in an adult body—reckless, aching, floating somewhere between detachment and self-destruction. I played invincible, but deep down, there were nights I silently hoped something would take me out. Quietly. Without explanation.

One of those nights—the kind where you stop caring who you're with or what happens—led to an unexpected pregnancy.

I remember staring at the test in disbelief, the air in the room growing thick, the walls somehow closing in. My heart didn't race. It sank.

Abortion was forbidden in the faith I was raised in. Even the thought of it brought on a shame so heavy, it felt like it could bury me. I believed if I chose that route, I'd be beyond redemption. That God would turn His face from me for good. That my already fractured relationship with my family—and with myself—would never recover.

Could I live with that kind of choice? Could I carry that weight forever?

I didn't think I could.

So I chose to carry the pregnancy.

To bring life into a world I barely wanted to live in.

I was terrified. Guilt-ridden. Ashamed. I felt irresponsible, careless, selfish. I felt like life had grabbed me by the collar and was dragging me forward whether I was ready or not.

So I made a deal with myself.

Just get through it.
Make enough money.
Give your daughter everything you never had.
And then . . . disappear.

That was my plan. I wasn't dreaming for myself anymore. I didn't make long-term plans that included my own joy or healing. I had already forfeited my own worth.

But carrying her gave me a reason to keep going—a sliver of purpose in a life that otherwise felt disposable.

She didn't save me all at once. But she gave me something to hold onto. A flicker. A thread. Just enough to push forward . . . a little while longer.

It took me becoming a mother to realize the gravity of what I didn't have.

And I realized it was easier for me to forgive my dad than it was to forgive my mom.

He left.
But she stayed.
She stayed . . . but not in the way I needed her to.

She was tired.
She was sick.
She was a grieving woman with a chronic illness, trying to hold together a world that had just collapsed.

She was barely surviving.

And I hated her for it.

I hated that she couldn't show up for me.
That she always seemed to get sick when I needed her the most—
Like when I gave birth to my first child.

CHAPTER 6

The Labor

*I*t was time to enter the real world. The workforce. I stumbled through a few jobs in the medical field—chasing titles I thought sounded impressive, trying on roles I thought might fit. But nothing clicked. I wasn't sure who I was or what I really wanted.

Before that, I had gone to school to become an auto body technician—drawn to the idea of fixing broken things, maybe hoping it would teach me how to fix myself. I shifted into cosmetology next, only for the school to shut down before I could finish. From there, I tried skincare, thinking maybe helping others feel beautiful would help me feel seen too.

But survival doesn't always leave room for alignment. I had to choose jobs that paid the bills, not ones that fed my spirit. I was always pivoting, always rebranding, trying to find a path that made sense—or at least made money.

And then, my uncle (my mama's younger brother) told me about a job opportunity to work for Consumers Energy. I didn't fully understand what the company even did at the time, or what kind of system I was walking into.

But it was a paycheck. A nice paycheck.

What I didn't realize then was that this wasn't just a job lead—it was an extension of the way my uncle had always tried to prepare me. He made sure I knew how to take care of myself. He taught me how to change a tire and check the oil, how to talk to mechanics without getting taken advantage of. He walked me through the basics of credit and introduced me to concepts like wealth-building and generational equity—things no one else around me was talking about.

At the time, his words felt like another language—foreign, layered, and too big for me to fully hold. But he kept repeating them. Planting seeds. Breaking things down. And eventually, years later, they started to bloom. He never spoke down to me, even when I didn't get it. He just kept teaching. And that kind of consistency? I didn't take it lightly.

He always kept it real with me. He told me straight up: "I'll never be your dad. I can't fill that role. But I'm here. Always."

And he meant it. I never doubted it. Not once.

That became so important to me—to show him that everything he poured into me mattered. I didn't want to disappoint him. I wanted to carry what he gave me with pride.

He encouraged me to speak up—to have an opinion, to question things, even when he didn't agree. And when I did speak, he listened. Sometimes he'd challenge me, respectfully, but he never made me feel small. He taught me how to read a room, how to pay attention to people's character—not just their words.

So, when he brought up the job, I listened. I trusted him. Even if I didn't yet trust myself.

✳

As a Gas-meter reader for Consumers Energy, I hauled myself mile after mile—pregnant and often sleep-deprived—through alleys, across backyards, down unfamiliar streets in cities I hadn't even known existed. Just miles from where I grew up, yet they felt like foreign territory.

I wasn't just walking—I was navigating, dodging loose gravel, broken fences, and whatever else the day decided to throw at me.

Sometimes, it was dogs—angry, barking, teeth-baring dogs. More than once, I realized a gate had been opened on purpose. Some people saw meter readers as intruders, and I was an easy target: a young Black woman, visibly pregnant, alone. I'd sprint out of yards, adrenaline masking the pain in my feet until hours later when I peeled off my boots and could barely stand.

There were days I got lost in unfamiliar neighborhoods, soaked to the bone in the pouring rain. My uniform clung to my skin, heavy with water, dirt, and despair.

I'd sit in the car between routes, windows fogged up, tears streaming down my face, trying to catch my breath. The heat inside the vehicle felt suffocating, but stepping outside meant more walking, more stares, more struggle.

I was working through more than just pregnancy—I was walking through the weight of everything I'd never had time to feel. Still, I didn't stop.

My mother would remind me:
"Be strong. Keep going. You don't get to fall apart now."

And so, I didn't. I wiped my face, swallowed the lump in my throat, and pushed through—one block, one meter, one mile at a time. The walking kept the weight down, but the cost wasn't physical.

Exhaustion had seeped into my soul.
My world shrank to a rhythm I couldn't break: sleep, work, OB appointments, repeat.
There was no room for softness, no time to feel the miracle growing inside me—just the demand to survive.

At that time in my life, choosing a doctor meant circling the first in-network name on my insurance list.
He was brisk, clinical—eyes fixed on the chart, never on me.

I didn't know prenatal care could be different; advocacy wasn't in my vocabulary. Doctors were supposed to care. Why would they do otherwise?

Late in the third trimester, my daughter's kicks faded. A cold dread spread under my sternum. At the next appointment I told the nurse, "She isn't moving. Something's wrong." She relayed the message.

The doctor stalked in without greeting, lifted my gown, and performed an internal check—no warning, no eye contact.

"You're almost out of amniotic fluid," he muttered, accusation threading his voice.

"What have you been doing?"

"I—I read gas meters. I walk all day. This is my first pregnancy— I'm not sure what's norm—"

"Order a fluid scan," he snapped at the nurse, already turning away.

Chaos bloomed: techs, stretchers, clipped phrases I could barely parse.

I sat frozen, an empty vessel housing a silent child, wondering if obedience to faith had cornered me into tragedy.

A new man appeared—tall, sterile, agitated. The anesthesiologist. He explained blood transfusion protocol, then glanced at the notation on my chart: No Blood Products—Religious Reasons.

His eyes sharpened.
"Let's be clear—you're willing to leave a newborn motherless?"

The question hit harder than any needle.
He saw the death wish I hid beneath doctrine.
Part of me did crave an exit—no more loneliness, no more hollow futures, just quiet nothingness.

I stayed silent.

Within minutes they wheeled me into surgery for an emergency C-section.

My Nanna was tending to my Mama in another hospital, her lupus flaring yet again.

Resentment flared in me: *She always gets sick when I need her.*
I felt childish and cruel for thinking it, but the thought landed anyway.

※

In the fluorescent glare of the OR, as scalpels met flesh, I half-hoped the monitors would flatline.
I was exhausted—emotionally hollow and physically wrecked.

Instead, a cry cut through the haze—thin, fierce, insistent.

It was an emergency C-section, and everything felt like it was happening to me, not with me. My great-aunts came to check on me afterward, cooing over my baby while I drifted in and out of a fog.

After they left, I tried to rest, but pain tore through me like a fresh blade. My daughter slept peacefully through the entire night, but I lay there, silently breaking. When I finally cried out, begging the nurses for pain meds, I was told I wasn't due for more yet. Down the hall, I could hear another woman groaning in labor—moaning openly, without shame.

I envied her noise.
My own pain was minimized, brushed aside with clinical indifference.

"You're fine," the nurse said, barely looking up.
But I wasn't fine.
I was bleeding, stitched, and trembling beneath the weight of a new life—still expected to carry it all.

This is the part they don't talk about: how Black women are seen as stronger, more tolerant of pain, more able to endure

without complaint.
But my strength was not a badge that night—it was a burden.
And I was tired. So tired.

I didn't know then that this quiet suffering wasn't rare—it was practically inherited, passed down like a cautionary tale dressed up as strength.

It felt like the first test of many: to prove myself worthy of help, of rest, of softness. And already, I was failing.

My daughter announced herself to a world I had wanted to escape. I didn't know it then, but her cry would become the first note in a long song toward radical self-love—a sound that pulled me, however reluctantly, back into life.

CHAPTER 7

The Breakdown

*I*t took years for me to realize how much I blamed myself for the pieces I couldn't control—how deeply I internalized my dad's absence as proof that something must've been wrong with me.

Grief doesn't leave just because we stop talking about it.

It all came to a head one afternoon while I was out reading meters. Just weeks after walking away from the water, I had been holding everything in—grief, confusion, exhaustion—and my body finally betrayed me. I broke down in the middle of my route.

I had been holding everything in for so long—moving through my shifts like a ghost, numbing out, pretending I was okay. But on that afternoon, something snapped. I sat trembling in my 2004 silver alero, and with shaking hands, I called the mental health hotline my job always promoted during our check-ins. *'If you or someone you know needs help . . . '* It was the only voice that had offered help in weeks. In that moment, it felt divine—like God was still watching, even if no one else was.

After a brief series of questions, they sent an ambulance to pick me up and take me to the hospital.

Once there, I was sedated—though I was already barely conscious, my thoughts scattered, my limbs heavy with exhaustion and fear. I remember the cold pinch of the needle, the blurred faces leaning over me, and the sting of surrender. I didn't resist. I couldn't.

When I finally opened my eyes, it was dark outside. The room was dimly lit by a flickering fluorescent light. Bars covered the windows, casting long, skeletal shadows across the tiled floor. The air was thick—not just with antiseptic and worn vinyl, but something else: shame, restraint, silence. It clung to the walls like invisible mold.

I sat up slowly, my body stiff, my mouth dry, my sense of time distorted. The walls were that dull institutional gray—the kind of color that neither soothes nor offends. There was nothing warm or human in the space. No clock. No mirror. Just a blinking red camera in the corner.

Panic settled over me like a weighted blanket.

The door creaked open, and a young Black woman walked in. Her presence was soft but assured. She wore a hospital badge and a tired smile—the kind you learn to wear when you've seen too much and still choose to show up.

She introduced herself as a social worker.

I didn't smile back. I was angry. Confused. My voice cracked as I snapped,

"Where is my stuff?"

The desperation in my tone betrayed me. I wasn't just asking about my phone or my purse—I was grasping for anything that could tether me to a version of myself that still made sense.

Her expression didn't shift much, but something softened in her eyes. She spoke gently, as if she understood I was fighting my way through the fog with whatever fragments of self I had left.

She read through her script like a protocol, but then her voice lowered. She leaned in and said something I'll never forget:

"You need to get it together. If you don't say the right things, they'll threaten to take your daughter. Do you understand?"

My stomach dropped.

Her words landed like both a lifeline and a warning shot.

I thought they were going to help me . . . not lock me away and threaten to take the only reason I had to live.

I nodded, numb, and agreed to counseling because I knew it was the only way they'd release me. But in that moment, something in me shifted. I didn't feel seen. I felt surveilled. Managed.

Controlled.

I walked out of that hospital with my mask stitched tighter than ever. I wasn't healed—I was hardened. And I did what I'd always done: shoved the pain deeper, showed up for my daughter, and kept going.

There was no room to grieve. No permission to fall apart. I had a child to raise and no one to catch me if I crumbled.

�֎

The first therapist on my insurance list was an older man. I sat across from him week after week, crying while he stared at me blankly. He never offered more than a nod or a dry, "And how did that make you feel?"

Eventually, I tried another therapist—an older woman who reminded me of an auntie. She gave practical advice, told me to hire help, encouraged me to rest—but I couldn't receive it.

I wasn't ready to hear solutions because I hadn't yet named the problem.

I kept showing up to therapy just to check a box. Insurance was covering it, so why not? But I wasn't there to heal. I was just trying not to drown.

The providers always offered the same standard questionnaires. I kept retelling the same stories about my mama, circling the same pain, never quite touching the root.

It wasn't that there weren't any good therapists out there—it's that I hadn't learned how to ask myself:

What do I actually need help with? What kind of healing am I even seeking?

I wasn't being intentional. I was surviving.

And the system? It didn't ask either.

So, I slipped through the cracks. Not because I didn't want to get better—but because no one ever paused long enough to ask the questions that might've helped me help myself.

Rooted Reflections: Your Turn

Section Two: Taking Root
Theme: Belief, Belonging, and Becoming

Scripture: Genesis 2:17

"But of the tree of the knowledge of good and evil, you shall not eat, for in the day that you eat from it you will certainly die."

Spiritual Insight:

In the garden, everything was whole — until humanity chose to judge rather than simply be. That moment of separation birthed shame, fear, and the illusion that we must hide or earn love. In many ways, we repeat that choice daily — eating from the tree of judgment, labeling ourselves as "too much," "not enough," or "unworthy."

But healing begins when we pause, get still, and return to Divine presence.

In stillness, we remember: we were never meant to carry shame. We were always meant to create — not from fear, but from connection.

• In what areas of my life have I been judging myself harshly?
• How has that judgment distanced me from who I truly am?
• What does it look like to return to stillness, to just be?

This section invites you to explore how your beliefs, upbringing, and environments shaped the roots of your identity. Whether you were raised in a strict religion, felt unseen in your family, or had to mask parts of yourself to be accepted—this is your space to reflect.

1. Who Told You Who You Had to Be?

Think back to the environments (family, school, religious spaces) where you learned what was expected of you.

• What were the spoken or unspoken rules?

• How did those rules impact how you showed up in the world?

✐ *Reflect below:*

_____

_____

_____

_____

_____

2. Invisible & Misunderstood

In this section, the author shared how her pain was minimized, labeled, or dismissed.

• Have you ever been called "too sensitive," "dramatic," or "rebellious" when you were actually hurting?

• How did people respond when you needed help?

• What did those responses teach you about expressing your emotions?

🖎 *Explore here:*

_____

_____

_____

_____

3. Faith, Fear & Conditional Love

If you grew up in a religious or rule-based environment:

- Were you taught that love was something you had to *earn or prove?*

- How did that shape your view of God, love, or self-worth?

🖎 *Journal below:*

_____

_____

_____

_____

4. Grief Without Language

This section also holds unspoken grief—the kind that hides in silence, disappointment, or spiritual exile.

- Is there grief in your story that was never named or validated?

- What would it sound like if you gave that grief a voice now?

✐ *Write from the heart:*

_____

_____

_____

_____

_____

5. What Are You Ready to Uproot?

Growth doesn't mean rushing to heal—it means getting honest about what no longer fits.

- What beliefs, behaviors, or identities are you ready to release?

- What truth about yourself are you finally ready to embrace?

✐ *Let your roots loosen. You are growing:*

_____

_____

_____

_____

SECTION THREE:

The Stem

Through the Concrete

CHAPTER 8

The Mirror of Motherhood

*Y*ears of chemical relaxers, cheap flat irons, and chronic dryness had left my hair brittle and broken. When the last bit of new growth refused to lie flat, I said goodbye to the creamy crack. But going natural didn't feel freeing—it felt risky. Like wandering outside the congregation's fence.

I still thought my real hair was too "loud," too much. So I kept it braided and tucked away beneath weave I hoped looked effortlessly "natural." I'd sit for hours in tiny African braiding shops—convinced that women from "the Motherland" must know how to care for our hair. And while they did braid fast, it came at a cost: every tight stitch snatched a little more of my edges, no matter how many they promised to "leave out." Each missing follicle felt like proof I should keep hiding, adding, covering. My hair—like my voice—wasn't allowed to take up space.

But holding my daughter cracked something open in me that religion never could.

It made me question: What do I want her life to look like?

And deeper still—why didn't I believe I deserved the same?

※

As the child of a teenage mother, I often felt more like her little sister than her daughter—caught in the limbo between being cared for and being expected to carry the weight. I grew up in the shadows of her exhaustion, learning early not to ask for too much, not to need too loudly.

At the time, I didn't understand her pain. Truthfully, I didn't want to.
It was easier to be angry. To stay focused on what I didn't receive.
And what I lacked hurt so deeply, I built a wall around my heart and called it strength.

But after becoming a mother myself, I started to see things differently. I began to realize that maybe she hadn't emotionally abandoned me—maybe she had just run out of capacity.

Grief, illness, disappointment . . . it had worn her down. She had been trying to survive the only way she knew how.

It took me becoming a mother to realize what I didn't have. But it took becoming an observer to recognize what she didn't have either.

She was sick.
She was grieving.
She was likely still battling her own childhood trauma—carrying weight no one ever helped her name.

And still, she did her best. Imperfectly. Inconsistently. But sincerely.

My mama was one of the pretty tomboys who loved everything about football—especially playing it —and the trumpet. She never let the world tell her who she was. The spirit of a rebel coursed through her . . . and then through me.

Just a few years after I was born, my mama's body began to betray her. And after my brother was born when I was two, her health declined even more.

Lupus waged a slow, invisible war inside her—stealing her energy, her mobility, and eventually, her sense of self. Some days, she couldn't get out of bed. Her joints ached. Her youth faded faster than it should've. Hospital stays grew longer. Smiles took more effort. She wore her exhaustion like a second skin.

I used to imagine her in a death match with the illness—desperately trying to hold on to her youth, her vigor, her life.

But it wasn't just the illness she was battling.

She was grieving too—the kind of grief no one ever really sees. She was mourning the life she thought she'd have. Mourning the loss of her first love, my father. Mourning the freedom that illness had stolen from her one flare-up at a time. And because she had to keep going—because she had two kids to raise—she didn't get to unravel. She just carried it all. Quietly. Desperately.

I used to think she should've done better.

Now I see that she was carrying a kind of pain I hadn't yet learned how to name.

Now I see she did the best she could with what she had.

And so, slowly, I softened.

I reached out more. Called her. Asked questions I had once avoided. I started to notice the places where she was trying too—stumbling through vulnerability in her own way. We weren't perfect. But there were moments: shared meals, gentle check-ins, laughter that didn't feel so forced.

Mother to mother, something in me was trying to forgive her.

I didn't know that time was running out.
That the window for healing was closing faster than I could catch it.

But I'm still grateful we had that window at all.

We never fully mended things—not in the way I had hoped.

And by the time I was finally ready to lean in and love her without all the weight of resentment, it was too late.

✳

I had just passed my advancement test at Consumers. I remember the rush of pride and disbelief as the instructor announced, "You passed," with a wide grin.

After years of survival mode, long days on foot reading meters, and doubting whether I was capable of more—I had done it.

I was moving into the service department, just like my mother had always pushed me to.

It should've been a moment of celebration.
But the celebration never came.

Because just as I was soaking in that long-awaited success...
I checked my phone.

A missed call.
And a simple text from my cousin:

"Call me back ASAP, it's important."

CHAPTER 9

The Last Time

$\mathcal{S}$he fought hard—until the very end.

My mom never took the time to explain her illness to me in detail. She never sat me down and walked me through what Lupus was doing to her body—what it meant to live with a chronic illness that attacked her from the inside out.

For a long time, I resented her for that. I mistook her silence for emotional distance. I thought, *If I had known more, I could've done more.*

But in time, I came to understand: it was her way of protecting me.

She didn't want me to carry her burden. She didn't want me worrying every time she winced in pain or canceled a plan. She wanted me to live freely, not in the shadow of her sickness. That was her form of love—quiet, selfless, and hidden beneath the surface.

⋇

When I turned eighteen, I made up my mind to try and donate a kidney to her. I wanted to do something—anything—to take the pain away. To prove my love in a language her body might understand. I remember telling her, expecting gratitude or relief.

But she was furious.

"I don't want nobody cutting on you," she snapped. Her tone was sharp, but her eyes were soft. It was one of the few moments I saw how deeply she loved me—not through affection or approval, but through fear. She couldn't bear the thought of me suffering, even for her.

Of course, I rebelled—just like I had throughout our mother-daughter relationship. It was always a dance between defiance and devotion, between trying to save her and trying to save myself.

But fate had other plans.

I wasn't a match.

Her body had developed antibodies against mine from carrying me in her womb. The irony still stings: the same closeness that once tethered us together in life was now the very thing preventing me from helping her stay alive.

I couldn't save her.

And sitting beside her hospital bed, holding her still hand, I was reminded of how helpless I had always felt in the face of her pain. How small I felt when I couldn't fix it. How being her daughter had always meant loving her without ever fully reaching her.

At that moment, all I could do was be there.

And maybe—just maybe—that was enough.

My mother never looked me in the eyes and said, *"I'm proud of you."* Her pride lived in her persistence. In the way she pushed me to stand on my own two feet, even as hers began to fail her.

Her love was quiet. Sometimes hard. Sometimes misdirected. But it was real.

She told me:
> "Create stability for Cailyn."
> "Be more merciful, Bri."

That day—what should have been a milestone—was shattered by loss.

It had already been hard trying to be there for her while she was in and out of the hospital. I'd been doing my best—driving back and forth from training in Flint to the hospital in Ann Arbor, exhausted and anxious with every mile.

I tried to explain to my job how serious her condition was, how critical those visits were—not for show, but because I needed to be there. But they didn't hear me. They assumed I was just trying to get paid for the drive.

Instead of listening, they gave me an ultimatum: stay in Flint to test, or risk being demoted back to meter reading.

Then came the phone call:

> "They're going to turn off the machine, but they're waiting for you to get here."

Everything after that felt like static.

I cried the entire drive to the hospital, screaming into the silence, gripping the steering wheel like it could somehow hold the weight of what I was about to lose.

Why now? Why this day?
The timing felt like a cruel joke. A punishment for something I hadn't even figured out yet.

When I arrived, the hospital room and lobby was already full— cousins, aunts, uncles, even my great-grandmother. My senses were flooded.

The sterile smell of antiseptic.
The hum of machines.
The low murmur of family.

I held her hand and said goodbye.

I told myself she was finally free. That she wasn't suffering anymore. That I was relieved.

But none of it felt true.

There was stillness in the room. A kind of silence that didn't feel peaceful—just final.

We all stood frozen, watching her chest stop rising. No beeps. No breath. Just a body that had carried so much now lying still.

My ears felt clogged, like I was underwater. The sounds around me—sniffles, gasps, someone sobbing—were muffled and far away. The only thing that cut through was a voice, repeating over and over:

"Call your brother. Call your brother and tell him."

I couldn't move. I couldn't think.
The words echoed in my head, but my hands didn't work.
How do you tell someone their mother is gone?

That conversation still haunts me.

I had to be the one to tell him. To break his heart with words I barely understood myself.

As his big sister, I was supposed to have the answers. I was supposed to be the strong one.

But at that moment, I failed him. And that failure settled somewhere deep inside me.

I don't remember what I said, only the sound of his silence. The way it stretched between us, thick with disbelief.
I've never stopped wondering if I could've said it differently.

Softer. Better.

But nothing softens news like that.

I don't remember who I called after that. I don't remember the walk out of the hospital, or how I made it home.

Grief does that—blurs the edges, wipes out the details, and replaces them with one sharp truth: she was gone.

The last time I held her alive, I was helping her down the stairs—her frail body leaning into mine. That was our last moment of shared strength. And I didn't know it would be.

What hurt more than anything was the guilt.
How little time I had spent trying to understand her.
And how much time I had spent resenting her.

CHAPTER 10

Her Humanity Set Me Free

My mother's funeral felt nothing like my father's. The service was held at the Kingdom Hall, but instead of a casket, there was a single, radiant photograph of her at the front—an image so full of life it almost made the room feel brighter.

I loved that part.

In the days leading up to the service, her closest cousins took charge of the arrangements, gently keeping me in the loop even though I floated through each conversation like a ghost. Calls poured in, texts buzzed nonstop, and I answered only when I could summon the energy—which was rare.

When the day arrived, I stepped into the Hall and was immediately cornered:

"Why haven't you picked up your phone?"
"We wanted to cook for you!"

"What's happening after the service? No one's telling us anything!"

One woman's voice cut through the murmur, sharp and accusing.

For half a second, I envisioned my fist meeting her perfectly powdered face—one of those cinematic flashes where the protagonist snaps, only to blink back to reality untouched. Instead, I swallowed the rage, forced a polite smile, and walked away.

We'd already decided: a private, family-only gathering afterward. No announcements. No open invitations.
I was grateful for that boundary.

❋

Despite our splintered beliefs, we could still close ranks when it mattered.
My mother's cousins—practically her little siblings—showed up in full force. She had looked after them even while battling her own storms, and now they returned the favor with quiet, unwavering presence.

In that moment, love looked like pans of food in the trunk, whispered check-ins, and a photo of my mother that proved a spirit can light up a room even when the body is gone.

※

Sitting with these truths hasn't been easy.

I used to cringe at that cliché: *She did the best she could with what she had.*
I thought it dismissed my pain.
I thought it implied that everything that happened to me could be excused or overshadowed by my mom's struggle.

But over the years, I've learned there is beauty in duality. More than one thing can be true at once.

That perspective set me free.

It allowed me to sit my hurt aside, even briefly, and acknowledge what *she* went through.
Then I picked my pain back up—but this time, I left blame and guilt out of the equation.

That's when the healing began.
I shed the pieces I no longer needed in order to become the woman I was choosing to become.

I stopped looking at her through the eyes of the child in me who needed more.
And I started seeing her through the lens of compassion.

I let myself grieve the mother I didn't have . . .

While honoring the woman she was—strong, soft, broken, and still trying.

Forgiveness didn't come overnight.
It came through presence.

Through allowing myself to feel it all without flinching.
Through talking about her with God.
With my children.
With you—right now, in these pages.

This is how I keep her—and my father—alive.

By telling their truth.

By acknowledging their humanity.

I set myself free—from what they couldn't give me

And it's my hope that in reading this, *you* choose to mend something, too.

Not just for the other person's sake—
But so you can be free.
So you can love deeply.
So you can finally taste the intimacy that pain tried to steal from you.

CHAPTER 11

Through the Concrete

*G*rief cracked me open in a way that meetings at the Kingdom Hall couldn't mend. And in that crack, something divine whispered—not from the literature, not from the platform, but from within me:

"There's more."

More than rules.
More than guilt.
More than fear-based obedience.
There's more to *me*.
There's more to *God*.
And there's more to life than surviving under the weight of *should*.

At some point, it got harder to pretend.
The scriptures I once read for guidance now felt like mirrors reflecting my guilt.

The meetings that once gave me comfort started to feel cold—like rituals I was performing just to keep from falling apart.

I still believed in God.
But I wasn't sure I believed in the system that told me how to reach God.

What made it harder was how much I had invested:
Years.
Friendships.
Identity.

People looked at me and saw someone strong in the faith—
reliable, obedient, committed.
But what they didn't see was how tired I was.
Tired of the performance.
Tired of constantly policing my thoughts.
Tired of feeling like I had to earn love, grace, or acceptance.

I didn't leave all at once.
I began tuning in more closely during the meetings.
And I asked myself:
Is this something I want for my daughter?

At first, I kept my questions to myself.
This was personal.
Sacred.
Mine.

It started with quiet conversations—usually the kind I would have avoided. People who described themselves as spiritual rather than religious. In the past, I might've challenged them, subtly trying to plant seeds of what I believed to be "truth." But this time, I did something completely opposite of what I had been taught: I listened. I didn't try to convert. I didn't judge. I simply observed.

Their relationship with God didn't sound like fear—it sounded like freedom. Like love.

Curious, I began to explore beyond the boundaries I once clung to. I picked up *The Alchemist*. Bought a journal on Stoicism. Not because I was trying to adopt a new identity or belief system, but because I wanted to understand. To see the world outside the lens of fear I had worn for so long.

I started researching. I looked up words I had once been told to avoid. I asked questions I was once afraid to speak. Not to rebel—but to be honest.

And with each new perspective, the fear began to loosen its grip

✳

And for the first time, I didn't feel condemned.
I felt *seen*.
Held.
Invited to return to myself.

I started releasing fear.
Stopped shrinking from questions.
And allowed myself to explore ideas not filtered through shame or control.

I started seeking truth that looked like *love*.
Messages rooted in support, grace, and connection.

And little by little . . .
I began building a relationship with God that didn't feel like punishment.

I didn't have to earn this love.
I didn't have to perform.
I just had to remember I was already *worthy* of it.

And that's when everything began to change.

I meditated on everything I'd learned and read—but still, I hesitated to act on what I was learning.
I feared being "led astray."

So I stayed.
Because the fear of leaving was stronger than the pain of staying.

Until it wasn't.

Something shifted the year my mother died.

Her death—sudden, heartbreaking, and final—brought me face-to-face with the reality I'd been avoiding:

I had spent most of my life trying to please a version of God that didn't look anything like *love*.

And this wasn't just about skipping meetings or quietly fading away.
I needed this break to be *clear*.
Intentional.
Not emotional. Not impulsive.

So I did what I knew had to be done.
I wrote a letter of dissociation.

CHAPTER 12

A Letter

The cursor blinked at me, a steady metronome in the silence of my room.

My fingers hovered over the keyboard, stiff with hesitation.
I had rehearsed this moment in my mind a thousand times, but now that it was here, the weight of it pressed down on me.

This letter—just a few paragraphs, just words on a screen—would end the life I had known for thirteen years.

For over a decade, I had lived by the rules.
I had silenced my doubts, swallowed my fear, and sacrificed my identity in the name of salvation.
Because I was told it was the only way to be worthy.
And I believed them.

They warned me about people like me—those who strayed.
Those who let "outside influences" poison their faith.
I had promised myself I would never be one of them.

But the more I learned and experienced, the harder it became to unsee the truth.
And the truth was: I wasn't free.
I had never been free.

My chest tightened.
Fear coiled around my ribs, whispering all the reasons I should stop.
I knew what this letter meant:
Dissociation.
Isolation.
Losing the only community I had ever known.

I would be labeled an apostate. A traitor. A cautionary tale.

Seven months had passed since my mother died.
Seven months of trying to understand what her absence meant.

Of sorting through the complicated grief of losing a woman I was bound to by blood but never fully connected with.

Her family line had introduced me to this religion.
And now I was preparing to walk away from it.

For the first time in my life, I had a clean slate.
No longer tethered to her expectations or the faith she had passed down.

Still, fear gripped me as I hovered over the keyboard.
What would my family think?
What would they say when they found out I had turned my back on everything we were raised to believe?

More than anything, I feared being alone.

But then again, I already knew loneliness.
I had felt it as a child with a mother too sick to be present.
As a teenager shaping myself into what the religion expected—even when it felt unnatural.
And in its rawest, cruelest form, I felt it when I lost both of my parents.

I had already survived some of life's deepest heartbreaks.
What more could I lose?

And then—ironically—I thought back to my father's funeral. To the moment my great-grandma stood for her beliefs with unwavering conviction, even if it meant going head-to-head with ten Goliaths in the flesh.

I placed my hands on the keyboard and began to type.

"To the elders of the congregation . . . "

The words poured out—steady and certain.

The fear was still there, but beneath it, something stronger had begun to take root.

By the time I reached the last sentence, I knew:
This was not just a resignation.
It was a declaration.
A quiet rebellion.
A first step toward something I had never truly known.

Freedom.

This decision wasn't just about me.

In the next room of our small yet cozy apartment, my daughter slept—small, innocent, untouched by the weight of the beliefs that had shaped my world.
She was only a year and a half old, but already I knew:
I wanted something different for her.

A childhood not ruled by fear.
A life where she could ask questions.
Explore.
Become her own person without guilt or shame.

I refused to let her grow up believing that love was conditional.
That acceptance came at the cost of authenticity.
That she had to fit inside a mold to be considered enough.

If I stayed, I knew what her future would look like.
Because it would be my past.

And I couldn't let that happen.

With that final thought, I hit send.
And just like that, the life I had clung to for years was over.

But for the first time, it felt like mine had finally begun.

The next day at work, doubt crept in. I questioned whether I had made a mistake. Fear gripped me, and for a moment, I wanted to turn back. I whispered a prayer, asking God for a sign— something to reassure me that I was on the right path.

That's when I started seeing sunflowers. One after another, they seemed to appear out of nowhere. But it was the last one that stopped me in my tracks. I was returning my truck to the yard, driving the same road I had traveled countless times before, when I noticed it—just one, standing tall in a spot I'd never seen it grow. It was facing me, it felt completely out of place, yet perfectly timed.

It made me smile. And with that smile came a wave of peace I couldn't explain.
Something whispered, *"You're going to be alright."*
And for reasons I still can't fully name, I believed it.

I had finally broken through the concrete laid down by fear, guilt, and silence.

I snapped a picture and went home.

⁂

Sometimes, what we call *faith* is really fear in disguise.

I wasn't growing closer to God.
I was just getting better at hiding the parts of myself I thought God would reject.

But real faith—the kind that transforms and liberates—doesn't demand your silence.

It invites your honesty.
It doesn't shrink you.
It expands you.

Religion was always a paradox for me—both a cage and a shield.
Its rules often felt like chains: no college, no "worldly" friends, no questions asked.

And yet, those same restrictions sometimes formed a hedge of protection when I was at my lowest.

While no one around me seemed to notice the depression hollowing me out, let me be clear: I'm not condemning Jehovah's Witnesses, or any faith. My anger toward the religion was born from painful experiences.

But pain isn't exclusive to one belief system.

Life offers its own share of heartache—and joy.

We can't always label those moments good or bad.
But we can choose what serves us, and release what doesn't.

That's the duality I've come to accept.

Even though that faith is no longer my home, I can still honor
those who remain within it. I can keep the wisdom it gave me
while laying down the fear that kept me small.

Those boundaries once stopped me from choices that might
have destroyed me—
Before I understood my worth.

Now, after learning to practice self-care instead of fear-based
obedience, I can peel away the parts that harmed me
And hold fast to the parts that heal.

In this way, the faith that once confined me—also, in its
imperfect mercy—kept me alive long enough
To discover a deeper freedom:

Loving myself fully—without judgment,
Without conditions—
And finally knowing **peace.**

Photo credit: Briana Cobb

CHAPTER 13

The Uproot

*A*fter leaving the religion, everything felt . . . quiet.
Not peaceful quiet—uncertain quiet.
The kind that creeps in after a storm.
The kind where you don't yet feel safe, but you know you're no longer in danger.
At first, I felt lost.

I didn't know who I was without all the rules.
Without the community.
Without the identity I had spent so long constructing.

I thought healing was a straight line.
That if I cried enough in therapy, journaled daily, and repeated the right affirmations, I'd start to feel lighter.
But I wasn't getting lighter.
I was just getting louder in the same rooms.

Still depressed.
Still overthinking.

Still spiritually and emotionally exhausted.

At some point, I realized—I wasn't healing.
I was coping professionally.

I followed every rule, checked every box, said all the "right"
things.
Outwardly, I looked like a model of resilience.
But inwardly, nothing was shifting.
My heart kept its distance.
My body stayed tense, bracing for the next blow.
My soul hovered above the deepest wounds, afraid to land.

I didn't see it then, but I had become a master at tiptoeing
around my own pain.

Real freedom, I learned, isn't just about exiting a system.
It's about reclaiming the space that silence used to fill—with
your own voice.

It meant:
Speaking up in rooms where I used to shrink.
Setting limits in relationships where I once over-functioned.
Refusing to stay "grateful" for jobs that underpaid and
overworked me.
And in motherhood, modeling what I rarely saw growing up:
Self-worth.
Boundaries.
Emotional safety.

The real test came when I had to advocate for myself—
Not just spiritually,
Not just emotionally,
But professionally.
And later,
Medically.

Roots don't just hold you down—they hold you steady
while you rise.

Rooted Reflections: Your Turn

Section Three: The Stem

(Rising Through the Concrete)

Theme: identity, inner conflict, reclaiming your voice and power

Scripture: Jeremiah 1:5

"Before I formed you in the womb I knew you, before you were born I set you apart . . . "

Spiritual Insight:

You are not a mistake. You are not your past, your pain, or your performance.

Your identity was established before your arrival — whole, worthy, and set apart.

In this section, we strip away the roles, the masks, the expectations, and the conditioning that made you forget.

Reclamation is sacred. This is your return.

- Who was I before the world told me who to be?
- What parts of me am I ready to reclaim?
- Where in my life am I being called to stand in my truth?

1. Grief & Generational Healing

What truth have you recently discovered about a parent or caregiver?
How can you honor their humanity *and* your own pain?

_____

_____

_____

_____

_____

2. Hair & Identity

How has your hair mirrored your self-worth or freedom journey?
What early messages about "acceptable" appearance still linger?

_____

_____

_____

_____

_____

3. Releasing Survival Mode

When did you notice you were no longer just surviving—but starting to live?
What belief, rule, or system have you had to walk away from?

_____

_____

_____

_____

_____

4. Faith Rooted in Love

What does your relationship with God/spirituality look like when it's rooted in love instead of fear?

Have you ever confused people-pleasing or religious performance with actual connection to the Divine?

_____

_____

_____

_____

_____

Chapter 1

5. Personal Uprising

Which part of your life are you ready to reclaim—time, voice, dreams, body?
Write a one-sentence (or longer) declaration of freedom:

_____

_____

_____

_____

_____

6. Actionable Self-Love

Choose one to focus on this week and jot your first step below:

- Create a budget that protects your joy and rest.

- Spend 20 minutes on a soul-nourishing activity.

- Rewrite one outdated belief with compassion.

- Set a boundary that safeguards your peace.

- Speak loving affirmations to your reflection.

My chosen action & first step:

_____

_____

_____

_____

_____

Remember: *You are not merely breaking free—you are rising through the concrete, one intentional root and bloom at a time.*

SECTION FOUR:

The Branches

CHAPTER 14

Room to Rise

*I*n the corporate world, my hair became its own battleground. I loved expressing creativity by switching it up—one week a sleek bob, the next Marley twists, then box braids. Oddly, those changes caused more stir than my actual workload. Coworkers asked how I could "make it look so different overnight," their curiosity edged with disbelief.

One morning, a technician glanced at my faux locs and announced, loud enough for the crew room to hear, "Looks like you've got a bird's nest on your head!" Laughter rippled. A few people gave me wide-eyed pity for having to hear it. I cracked a joke back—quick, deflecting—anything to avoid the "angry, sensitive Black girl" label.

Inside, I was furious. I should've pushed back—for the culture and for myself. But in that moment, survival felt safer than confrontation.

Around that time, I decided to do the Big Chop. Years of tight braids—and one disastrous salon visit where an African braider sealed synthetic hair with a lighter—had fused plastic into my strands. When I took the style down, handfuls of hair hit the bathroom floor. I stood there sobbing, yet oddly relieved: if corporate America insisted on policing my crown, I would reclaim it on my own terms. I sheared everything to a close crop—fresh coils, fresh start—a quiet declaration that my value wasn't tied to length, conformity, or anyone else's comfort.

※

I'd poured thousands of hours into Consumers Energy. For several years as a first responder, I'd been grinding through mandatory 24/7 on-call assignments. I was often the first person on the scene—sometimes even before the fire department. My job required me to travel long distances in the dead of night, entering strangers' homes to investigate suspected gas leaks. More than once, what people thought was gas turned out to be spoiled food or unwashed dishes. It was draining—physically, mentally, and emotionally.

And yet, I learned more than I could've imagined. When I started, I didn't know what an elbow fitting was. I had never held half the tools I was suddenly expected to master. My coworkers weren't being paid to teach me—but so many of them did. Black men and women in the field took me under their wing, showing me how to work smarter, safer, and with confidence. That, paired with the grit and work ethic my mother instilled in me, made me one of the hardest-working technicians there. My photos are still showcased in the company's materials to this day.

Believing hard work alone would open doors. Temporary leadership assignments? Check. Resume? Polished and peer-reviewed. Corporate mentor? Committees? Continuing education? Check, check, check.

Colleagues assured me I was "a shoo-in" for promotion from the field to leadership—until the tone changed.

Suddenly, the air grew thick with unspoken questions: Who do you think you are?

I met it with diplomacy. "What else can I do?" I asked—because I was willing to do whatever it took.

Older colleagues—women and men who had navigated the system long enough to know its traps—quietly took me under their wings. I was soft-spoken, observant, always listening, so they poured wisdom into me like water into dry soil.

They taught me how to read between the lines of an email. How to decipher the political chessboard I didn't know I was standing on. How to speak with presence in a room full of decision-makers. How to assert without aggression. How to protect myself with language that couldn't be weaponized.

I didn't always know how to receive it. My guard was still high back then. Distrust sat in my chest like a stone, always reminding me not to get too comfortable, not to believe too deeply in good intentions.

But looking back now, I see how essential they were.

They invited me into spaces I wouldn't have entered on my own. They pulled up a seat when I might have eaten alone. They uplifted me—not because they had to, but because they wanted to see me win. That kind of support felt unfamiliar, almost suspicious . . . but it was real.

They showed me a different version of success—not just climbing the ladder, but staying rooted while you do.

Then the recruiter called—a brand-new gatekeeper.

He said he had "some advice."

"Your initial interviews give off angry Black woman vibes."

I guess he thought that, because he was a Black man, it was okay to say that to me. As if proximity to my experience gave him permission to weaponize it.

I swallowed the insult, thanked him for the 'feedback,' and kept applying.

After weeks of preparation, I finally made it past the gatekeeping. I landed an interview with a hiring manager who was excited and had heard great things about me—only to have her call the day before and say the position had been "eliminated." Not filled. Eliminated.

My colleagues urged me to keep trying.

✺

That season planted something in me. I began to understand the power of community—not just receiving it but eventually offering it. I wanted to be the kind of mentor I never knew I needed. Someone who could reach back, speak up, and help others navigate spaces that were never designed with us in mind.

Because even with their support, I was learning—painfully— that being good, prepared, or deserving didn't always protect you from being misread.

Microaggressions at work. Promotions yanked away. Hair falling out in clumps.

Each episode nudged me closer to a truth I could no longer ignore: the systems I trusted would not protect me. They could polish me, but not promote me. Tame me, but not honor me.

✺

I started drafting an exit plan toward entrepreneurship—where my work, my voice, and my hair could exist without apology.

But just as I was reclaiming my voice in the workplace, my body became its own battleground.

The stress I had swallowed for years—the suppressed rage, the invisible labor, the constant pressure to perform—had nowhere left to go. And it started to speak in ways I couldn't ignore.

I miscarried.

⁂

It happened quietly—without warning, without ceremony. One day I was pushing through the exhaustion, showing up to a job that rarely saw me as human, just capable. The next, I was bleeding out the hope I had barely dared to name. I had been so focused on proving my strength—to my employer, to myself—that I ignored the signs my body had been whispering for weeks. The mounting fatigue. The aches I waved off. The stress that clung to my shoulders like armor. I was still clocking in, still climbing into utility trucks at dawn, still mounting heavy meter stands, still entering strangers' homes at 2 a.m. to sniff out "possible gas" that often turned out to be nothing at all. And in the middle of that grind, something sacred slipped away from me.

The grief was layered. It wasn't just the loss of a child—it was the realization that I had once again sacrificed myself on the altar of survival. That the systems around me—medical, corporate, union—had not only failed to protect me but had expected me to carry it all in silence. I wanted to scream, but I didn't have the energy. I wanted comfort, but I was too ashamed to ask. Instead, I folded into the only thing I knew: keep going.

But something in me changed. The miscarriage became a quiet breaking point. A whispered warning from my body that it could no longer carry what my mouth refused to name. I knew then that if I didn't find another way to live—on my terms—I wouldn't survive the life I was trying so hard to maintain.

The loss devastated me. But it also re-ignited my resolve: the next pregnancy would be different.

When I conceived again, I chose my OB with intention and looped in my field leader early. I even secured a doctor's note outlining weight-lifting limits—proof I was ready to work, just safely.

✼

At seven months, the pelvic pain spiked. I requested light duty, exactly as policy allowed.

My field leader balked. "Why?" she asked, as if we hadn't discussed it for months. She fixated on one line—"No poisonous fumes."

"We need your doctor to clarify that gas isn't poisonous," she insisted.

I reminded her: in our own training, we were told gas wasn't poisonous—otherwise, we'd need protective gear. Her request wasn't just inappropriate. It was absurd.

My OB echoed the same: "I'm not a gas expert. They are."

Still, the supervisor threatened unpaid leave unless the note was rewritten.

The union shrugged it off—more than once. "Work it out with the field leader," they said.

Instead of representing me, they handed the burden right back. The very people paid to advocate on my behalf offered silence.

Only after my doctor sent an email calling their demands "borderline harassment" did they finally approve light duty.

✻

Those experiences—gatekeeping disguised as coaching, pregnancy treated like an inconvenience, advocacy labeled as attitude—became my breaking point and my breakthrough.

They showed me that the structures I trusted could not, or would not, protect me.

So I returned to sketching an exit plan—one that led to entrepreneurship, where my worth wouldn't be up for debate.

I was no longer waiting for a seat at their table—I was building my own.

CHAPTER 15

Do It Scared

*L*eaving was terrifying, but by then I'd learned the lesson my newfound faith had only begun to teach: real freedom is loving myself without conditions—speaking up where I once stayed silent, and building a life where my voice is not just heard, but welcomed.

After months of listening to gatekeepers mispronounce my value—of coded comments, mishandled pregnancies, and a steady hush around my worth—I knew I couldn't stay. I'd spent years proving myself to a system never designed to hold me, let alone celebrate me. So I stopped asking for permission and decided to build something of my own.

※

Night after night, once the kids were asleep, I sat at the kitchen table with a laptop, my phone, pen and paper—combing through articles on LLC formation and IRS codes, dog-earring every business and wealth-building book I could borrow. I researched how to open and manage a business bank account, how to apply for an EIN, and how to build a financial system I'd never been taught to believe I deserved.

I didn't yet know what I would use all of this for exactly—only that I needed the scaffolding ready when my purpose finally introduced itself.

During the day, I was learning how to be a mother without having one.
Self-parenting meant crowdsourcing wisdom: I joined Mommy & Me groups, asked countless questions at well-child visits, and Googled every concern with an urgency that only a mother who's both learning and healing can understand.

I needed answers. I needed community. Especially when my daughter's delicate nape began thinning, I vowed she wouldn't inherit my hair traumas—chemical burns, tight braids, self-erasing extensions. I turned to a sister-friend who'd done my own hair with gentleness and care. She taught me how to section tiny two-strand twists, how to mix oils for growth, and how to read my daughter's curls like they were Scripture.

The twists grew into budding locs. Months later, when I asked my daughter if she wanted to comb them out, she beamed.
"No, Mommy. I like them like this."
Her acceptance of her natural crown lit something in me.

I began searching for a stylist to maintain her locs, but every salon I visited felt rushed, unprofessional, or entirely uninterested in scalp health.

Frustrated, I decided to try my hand at the task myself. The first time I retwisted her roots —hands steady, heart thudding with purpose—I realized: this was it. I loved this work. Honoring textured hair. Pouring affirmation into people who'd been taught to hide their crowns.

From that epiphany, **Na'Truely Crown'd** was born. I filed the paperwork, sketched a logo in my notebook, chose brand colors, and drafted policies that centered rest, kindness, and consent.

Then I jumped.

I applied to work at a salon where my daughter had her hair done before, gaining experience for almost a year. Later, I transitioned to a salon closer to home that offered training, certification, and room to grow.

It was a community I didn't know existed—a young Black woman who had poured her all into building something of her own and was now reaching back to help others rise. I was amazed. Inspired.

✳

I walked away from a job on the cusp of paying me $40 an hour—steady money, yes, but at the expense of my mental health and self-respect.

The leave wasn't easy. I had discussed it with my husband, and he agreed to support me through the transition. I had always been good with saving and budgeting, and at this point, survival was second nature. I knew how to thrive with nothing—it was a language I'd long since learned to speak. Around that time, I was introduced to a financial mentor—who liked to call himself "The Financial Guru." He taught me how money actually works, how to set it up for success instead of cycling through it like we're conditioned to. I took out a loan from my 401(k) and used it as a cushion while I began building my clientele. I set a goal for how much I wanted to earn and showed up to the salon every day, even when I had no clients. I filled those slow hours by reading *Rich Dad Poor Dad* and *The Four Agreements*, soaking up wisdom, staying ready. I observed the other women in the salon, watched how they worked, how they moved. I even looked forward to the most challenging clients—I was just grateful to no longer be running from dogs, working in rain and snow, or navigating strangers' homes at odd hours of the night. Just being able to stay home at night felt like a luxury.

※

Entrepreneurship became more than a career move; it was a reclamation. I was crafting a space where I didn't have to code-switch or shrink—where culture, voice, boundaries, and vision could breathe in full color.

Yet even as I built a business rooted in freedom, my body was still learning what freedom felt like. I could speak life into clients, curate healing atmospheres, preach self-love—yet still flinch when my daughter flung her arms around my waist.

Leaving a system is one kind of liberation.
Receiving love is another entirely.

And that second revolution was still waiting for me—nestled in the tiny, insistent arms of my children.
Freedom in business arrived first.
Freedom in my body took longer.

CHAPTER 16

A Wound Without Edges

Disclaimer: This chapter reflects my personal mental health journey and is not intended as medical advice. Always consult with a licensed professional for diagnosis, treatment, or mental health support tailored to your individual needs.

✖

*I*n October of 2023—eight years after my breakdown and hospitalization, and three years after giving birth to my son—I found myself struggling to sleep. I sought help and was prescribed medication, but I was never told the full story: that I had been misdiagnosed as bipolar.

The therapist I had been seeing on and off for years—an older woman I trusted—referred me to a psychiatrist after I shared that I was experiencing hallucinations.

Not long after, she retired. And I was left alone to navigate what came next.

The psychiatrist prescribed sleep medication. It worked for a while, but I didn't fully understand what was happening. No one explained much. I was simply told to find a new counselor.

So I did—but this time, I approached it differently.

I came prepared. I made a list of questions, wrote down therapy goals, and researched providers through my insurance. I read reviews and took notes, trying to find someone who felt aligned.

One therapist I liked didn't take my insurance, but after hearing my story, she paused and asked, "That doesn't sound right. You were prescribed meds without a formal diagnosis?"

That one question changed everything.

She referred me to another counselor—the one I would eventually stay with.

After our first few sessions, that counselor echoed the same concern: no formal diagnosis had ever been communicated to me. She encouraged me to reach out to the psychiatrist directly.

I did.

He casually confirmed that no diagnosis had been shared and that the medication was "just to help me sleep."

Still, something didn't sit right.

I requested my medical records.

When they arrived, I sat with them—squinting through scribbles and codes, Googling terms I didn't understand. And there it was: *Bipolar Disorder*—written in messy handwriting, like a label carelessly slapped on me without so much as a conversation.

My new therapist, calm and professional, drafted a respectful letter challenging the diagnosis. She conducted her own assessments—something no one else had ever done. And through that process, she identified what I had quietly suspected all along: it wasn't bipolar.

It was adult ADHD.

I was prescribed ADHD medication shortly after. And for the first time in years, I could focus.

My mind slowed down.

I began to understand what calm actually felt like—not as an idea, but as an embodied reality.

I slept. Deeply.

And my mood lifted.

But per my goals, my treatment didn't rely on medication alone.

She taught me how to sit with my emotions.

How to trace them back to where they lived in my body.

How to name them without fear.

I learned to meditate.

And slowly, I began to feel relief—not just the absence of pain, but the presence of peace.

Eventually, I chose to stop the medication out of concern for long-term liver effects. I experienced mild withdrawal, but I wasn't afraid. I had something I never had before: a reference point.

I now knew what peace felt like. And that knowing couldn't be taken from me.

※

One day, while unraveling yet another thread from my past, I mentioned my father for the first time in therapy.

I hadn't even said his name in that setting before.

There's something that happens when your father dies before

you even understand what fathers are meant to be.

The grief doesn't land all at once.

It comes in fragments.

In milestones he missed.

In the silence when someone asks, "Who walked you down the aisle?"

In the ache of watching your own children and wondering, *What would he have been like with them?*

My father's death wasn't just a loss.

It was a void.

A wound without edges.

It buried itself—
In the silence.
In my body.
In the years I spent pretending I had "moved forward" just because I wasn't falling apart on the outside.

For most of my life, I thought that because I could function, I was fine.

But I was emotionally limping—protecting something I didn't even know still hurt.

✳

My therapist sat with it. Then gently said, "Write him a letter."

At first, it felt silly. But that suggestion—simple, almost dismissible—became the key to a door I hadn't dared approach.

She told me not to filter it. Not to make it poetic or spiritual or polished.

Just to write from my truth.

Say what I needed to say.

What I never got to say.

I rolled my eyes.

But something in me knew I had nothing left to lose.

So I did it.

✳

I sat with the silence.
Put pen to paper.

And as I wrote, I wept.

Not the quiet tears of adult sadness.

The deep, guttural sobs of the ten-year-old in me who never got to ask why.

Who never got to say goodbye.
Who never got to be angry . . . or confused . . . or scared out loud.

In that letter, I acknowledged his humanity.

I forgave him—not because I had to, but because I was ready.

I released what I had carried for too long.

And unexpectedly...
I felt connected to him.

Facing grief didn't shatter me.

It freed me.

It helped me finally move—not just forward, but *through.*

✳

Finding a therapist when you're already buried under life's pressures can feel like trying to climb out of quicksand barefoot.

It takes time. It takes energy you barely have. And the process—telling your story over and over again to strangers, answering intake questions like *"What brings you here?"* or *"When did the symptoms start?"*—can feel like re-opening wounds you never had time to clean properly. The truth is, when you're clouded by trauma, loss, and pain, clarity can feel like a luxury. The unknown is terrifying when you've spent years trying to stay one step ahead of your next heartbreak. That's why I want to offer this: it's okay to not have all the answers right away. In one of my lowest moments, I sat down and wrote just one small goal to share with my new therapist. That goal became my compass. And when I didn't know how to respond to a question, I gave myself permission to say, "I don't know the answer to that yet, but I'm here to figure it out. Do you have any tools that could help me find it?" Healing starts when we stop pretending we're supposed to know everything. Let yourself be helped. Let yourself heal.

Because avoiding pain doesn't protect us.
It keeps us stuck.

And healing doesn't always come in grand revelations.

Sometimes, it starts with a quiet letter...
To someone who will never read it—
But whose absence still shapes the pages of our lives.

That letter didn't fix everything.

But it cracked something open.

And when that crack formed, light got in.

A light that made it impossible to ignore how much I had internalized—
Not just my father's absence,
But my mother's pain too.

CHAPTER 17

The Echo of What Wasn't Said

*P*hysical touch was never my default love language. But my daughter—thick curls, bright almond-brown eyes, a laugh that could melt granite—had a need for affection that felt bottomless. She wanted hugs that lingered. Arms wrapped tight. The kind that whispered "I'm safe" when I'm on your chest.

Each time her little arms reached for me, something inside me stiffened.

Not because I didn't love her. I loved her fiercely.

But my nervous system had been trained to pair closeness with unpredictability, abandonment, or guilt. One hug felt like it drained a day's worth of energy. The more she asked, the more I shrank— annoyed with her, furious with myself for being annoyed.

So, I rationed intimacy.

Meals, stories, baths: yes. Long hugs: only when I could spare them—like affection was a paycheck I might overdraw. Deep down, I feared if I gave too much, I'd disappear.

When my son arrived, the pattern started repeating. One night, sitting on the edge of the bed, I felt the familiar overwhelm— tight throat, buzzing skin, guilt. This time, I refused to hand the pattern to another child. I named it out loud:

My body is flinching at love.

Therapy helped me listen beneath the flinch. Weeks of gentle digging revealed the truth: my children's hugs weren't just affection; they were invitations to be present. To be vulnerable. To be seen.

And I had spent my whole childhood mastering invisibility.

"Parentified," my counselor said softly.

The word cracked something open. I had been low maintenance for so long I mistook it for personality. But I did need. I needed a lot—and that terrified me.

I let the hidden girl speak at last: The one who spilled juice and felt shame for days. The one who swallowed hunger so no one would be inconvenienced. The one who hid under quilts with questions no one answered.

I ugly-cried while my counselor simply witnessed. No fixing. No shushing. Silence, this time, was safe.

Once seen, I could choose differently. I let my kids hug me one second longer than felt natural. Then two. Then three. I began offering a hug before they asked, breathing through the discomfort until it softened into joy.

On days I was touched out, I modeled something I'd never seen growing up: "Mommy's body is tired, but I love you. Let's snuggle later."

They understood. They learned not just how to receive love, but how to protect it.

In the end, it was never just about hugs. It was about answering the echoes of words I never heard: You're safe here. Your needs aren't too much. I want to hold you—even when you're messy.

Love, when you've grown up emotionally starved, can feel like too much. But it's only too much because it's unfamiliar. And unfamiliar things often feel unsafe—even when they are exactly what we've craved all along.

What I didn't realize for years was how deeply trauma and grief had shaped my nervous system.
I thought I was just tired. Just anxious. Just "wired this way."

But my inability to rest, to focus, to create with ease—it wasn't laziness or lack of discipline.
It was my body, still stuck in survival mode.

It was one of our last therapy sessions. My counselor—who had witnessed me unravel, rebuild, and rise—was beaming. Her energy hummed with peace.

We sat in silence for a while, meditating with the lights dimmed, the room thick with calm. When we came out of it, she hesitated. I could see the pause in her body before she spoke.

"There's something I want to share with you," she said slowly. "It might sound . . . crazy."

I almost laughed. At that point, there wasn't much that could scare me. "Go ahead," I told her. "I can handle it."

She looked at me, eyes soft and full. "I saw an image while we were meditating. A closed flower . . . and then, it opened." She took a breath. "It was you. You were the flower."

That simple, heartfelt vision cracked something open in me. I hadn't cried that many tears of joy in a session before. Not because of what she saw—but because I could feel the truth of it.

I was blooming. Maybe not all at once. But definitely, undeniably, becoming.

For so long, I poured everything I had into surviving. Then I became a mother—and suddenly, I was pouring into someone else.

I learned to tend to my daughter's hair like a garden. I studied textures, products, rhythms. I twisted and styled her locs with care and affirmed her reflection before she could question it.

"You're beautiful. Your hair is magic." I said the words out loud, even when I was still learning to believe them for myself.

One day, in the middle of a wash day ritual, I caught my reflection in the mirror—my own hair tied up, neglected, an afterthought.

It hit me: I was teaching her to love herself while quietly abandoning my own crown.

That was the day I decided to loc my hair.

Not because it was trendy. Not because I needed a new look. But because I was ready to commit to something—and someone—I had overlooked for years: me.

Starting locs was a sacred pause.
Each twist was an anchor.
Each retwist, a return to me.

Locs required patience. They demanded acceptance. I didn't want the shortcuts, or the hiding from the in-between stages.

I chose to surrender the illusion of control and learn to trust the process.

In many ways, my hair became my teacher.

And as my crown thickened, so did my perspective.

I used to judge my life in harsh absolutes—what went wrong, what I lacked, what hurt too much to name.

But healing began when I stopped labeling every moment as good or bad, right or wrong. I started watching my life like I watched my children sleep—softly, curiously, without expectation.

I became the observer.

I watched pain rise and fall like waves.
I noticed joy hiding in small places.
I stopped asking, "Why did this happen to me?" and started wondering, "What is this showing me?"

The shift was small, but it changed everything.

✴

Perspective is what gave my story new meaning.
I had been through abandonment, religious trauma, loss,
confusion, survival mode—but I hadn't been destroyed.

I had been reshaped.

There is no timeline for becoming whole.
But there is power in finally saying:

I deserve to be poured into, too.
Not because I've reached a milestone.
Not because I've proven my worth.
But because I exist. Because I've lived. Because I'm still here.

My children taught me how to nurture.
My hair reminded me to be present.
And my therapist? She reminded me that even the most tightly
closed flower will bloom—when it's ready, and not a moment
too soon.

※

The day I loc'd my hair, I didn't just start a new style—I made a
quiet vow:

No more neglecting myself to keep others comfortable.

What began as a commitment to care for my crown became a
ripple effect across every part of my life.

At first, I just felt . . . clearer. Lighter.

Y'all, I could walk outside in the rain!

Like I could hear myself for the first time in years. I noticed how differently I showed up in my business—more grounded, more honest about what I needed, more unapologetic about what I deserved.

I stopped performing for clients who didn't respect my time or energy.
I raised my prices.
I started attracting people who valued the experience I offered—not just the service.

Locs gave me permission to take up space.
And in that space, I began to dream again.

※

But something deeper was happening too.

I had spent years in survival mode—always hustling, constantly overextending, endlessly waiting for the next emergency.

I hadn't realized how much I had normalized exhaustion.
I was operating from the bottom of Maslow's Hierarchy of needs, just trying to secure food, shelter, and safety. I had spent

so long focused on the base of Maslow's Hierarchy—survival—
that I forgot there was more. Safety and stability were all I had
the capacity to chase.

I came to understand this more clearly while taking courses
on trauma.
As I learned how the nervous system stores pain, how
dysregulation becomes a way of life,
I saw myself in every module. Every lecture named something I
hadn't had words for.
And more than that—it gave me tools.

I combined what I was learning with the tools I gained from
therapy.

I began to pause more. To breathe.
To listen to what my body was saying without judging it.
I began meditating—not just to "calm down," but to come home
to myself.

When fear rose, I didn't shame it. I witnessed it.
I reminded myself: You are safe now. You don't have to brace
anymore.

And in that space, I began to *choose* again:

Joy instead of fear.
Presence instead of panic.
Gratitude instead of lack.

I stopped living on autopilot—replaying grief, reenacting lack.
And the more I focused on what was good, what was true,
what was possible . . .
The more goodness came my way.
Not because life stopped being hard,
But because I had stopped being at war with it.

Healing made space for more: for love, for belonging, for
confidence. Eventually, I reached the top of the pyramid—self-
actualization—not in the form of perfection, but in the freedom
to dream, create, and simply be.

I wasn't trying to become a new woman.

I was finally letting myself be the woman I already was.

I started talking to God in the quiet moments—not begging for
rescue but relating.
Meditating. Sitting still. Asking better questions.
I used to pray out of fear.
Now I commune with curiosity.
I stopped chasing signs and started trusting the knowing
inside me.

※

I stopped giving out of obligation and started re-evaluating my
entire relationship with love.

I stopped proving.
I started receiving.
I became intentional about who I let into my world.

My friendships shifted. My conversations deepened.

And because I was no longer trying to carry everyone, I could finally show up for those who needed me most.

I created a soft, supportive home.
I became a safe space for my children.
I became a better friend.

And then, something powerful happened:

I looked around and realized I had enough to give.
Not just leftovers—but overflow.

I became an advocate. I joined the board of a nonprofit foundation for survivors of trauma and grief. I didn't just speak from wounds—I spoke from wisdom.

I enrolled in more courses on mental health.
I signed up for a Harvard online class on leadership—not to add titles, but to return to the page with new tools to rewrite my story.

My creativity exploded.
My vision stretched.

My healing work deepened.

For the first time, I didn't feel limited by my pain.
I felt equipped by it.

My story wasn't a chain—it was a key.

The more I invested in becoming whole, the more I saw how limitless I already was.

Rooted Reflections: Your Turn

Section Four: The Branches

Theme: Relationships, grief, motherhood, entrepreneurship, transformation

Scripture: Isaiah 61:3

"To bestow on them a crown of beauty instead of ashes, the oil of joy instead of mourning . . . "

Spiritual Insight:

This part of the journey is messy and miraculous. It's where we rise with tear-stained faces and outstretched hands, building something beautiful from what once broke us.

God exchanges what we thought was lost for something sacred: wisdom, purpose, healing, and joy.

You are not just surviving anymore — you are blooming.

Rooted Reflection Prompts:

- What ashes have I risen from?

- How have grief and loss shaped my growth?

- In what ways am I becoming a crown of beauty?

This section explored how clarity, boundaries, and internal healing can shift how we show up in the world. As you reflect, let these prompts guide you in noticing your own patterns, breakthroughs, and possibilities.

1. What is something you once accepted as "normal" that you now recognize as survival mode?

What signs told you it was time to shift?

_____

_____

_____

2. Who or what in your life reminds you to bloom—especially when you're tempted to shrink?

What helps you stay rooted in your truth?

_____

_____

_____

3. What does a life designed for peace—not just survival—look like for you?

What simple rituals (like journaling, walking, or rest) can you commit to this month?

_____

_____

_____

4. Write a short letter to a younger version of yourself who didn't yet know they were worthy of love, rest, and support.

What would you want them to know now?

_____

_____

_____

5. What is one boundary or belief you're ready to redefine so that you can give and receive love more freely?

_____

_____

_____

Remember: growth doesn't always look loud. Sometimes, it's the quiet choice to show up differently. To bloom, even when no one's watching

SECTION FIVE:

The Bloom

CHAPTER 18

Fruit

I started this journey asking to be a millionaire. I thought the answer would come in dollars and status. But God responded with something far more generous: **God gave me back to myself.**

Not all at once.
Not without resistance.
But piece by piece.

By having me pause and reflect on everything I've come through in this life.

I used to think success looked like someone else's stage. Now I know success is walking into a room as my full self— hair in coils or cut close, voice steady, soul intact.

Success has been learning how to mother without a mother. It was choosing not to harden, even when life's unanswered questions gave me every reason to.

It was holding space for my children's softness while relearning my own.

Over time, all that emptiness became a kind of invitation.
I began to ask different questions.
Not "What should I believe?" but—

"Who am I without fear?"
"What do I truly value?"
"What does my relationship with God look like when no one else is watching?"

And slowly, I started to build a new relationship with God—
one based on intimacy, not instruction.
No longer a performance.
No longer an obligation.
Just presence.

I talk to God as my closest friend.
I ask questions and don't feel bad for not having the answers right away.
I listen.
I cry.

I stopped trying to "pray right" and instead let my life become the prayer.

It wasn't always neat or pretty.
Some days, I felt like I had nothing to stand on.

Other days, I felt more spiritually grounded than I ever had before.

But in that in-between space, something sacred happened:

I met myself.

The version of me that had been buried under the weight of who I thought I had to be.
The version of me who didn't just want to survive, but to thrive—
to create, to lead, to nurture, to speak.
And most importantly...
to live in alignment with truth—not just tradition.

The real richness?
Creating spaces where other people remember their worth too.

Through every workshop, every course, every conversation, I am living proof that:

You can break generational silence without breaking your spirit.
You can create a life that reflects your healing, not your hiding.

I didn't write this book to prove I'm strong.
I wrote it to remember I'm whole.

Whole doesn't mean flawless.
It means I stopped disowning the parts of me that were

inconvenient or misunderstood.
It means I chose to love:
the girl who cried quietly in corners,
the woman who flinched at hugs,
the mother who is still learning as she goes,
the young woman who bravely chose to walk away from the
water that day.

The life I longed for was never as far as I thought.

It was always on the other side of permission:
To grieve.
To leave.
To unlearn.
To ask.
To receive.
To become.
To Rise Through the Concrete.

Rooted Reflections: Your Turn

Section Four: The Bloom

Theme: Legacy, impact, spiritual wholeness, leadership

Scripture: John 15:5

"I am the vine; you are the branches. If you remain in me and I in you, you will bear much fruit..."

Spiritual Insight:

You are bearing fruit not because you worked harder — but because you chose to stay connected.

Legacy is not about perfection — it's about presence. It's about staying rooted in your Source and trusting the unfolding.

You don't have to prove your worth anymore. Just be who you were always created to be. The seeds you're planting now? They will feed generations.

Rooted Reflection Prompts:

- What fruit am I producing in this season of my life?

- How am I staying connected to what truly matters?

- What legacy do I want to leave behind?

A soft landing. A sacred beginning.

Use this space to reflect on your own journey through the concrete. These questions aren't meant to be answered perfectly—they're meant to be lived into, over time.

What am I ready to reclaim?

_____

_____

_____

_____

Where am I being invited to begin again?

_____

_____

_____

_____

What legacy do I want to leave behind?

_____

_____

_____

_____

Who am I becoming when I stop shrinking to survive and start expanding to thrive?

_____

_____

_____

_____

If my life became the prayer—what would it say?

_____

_____

_____

_____

EPILOGUE

Legacy Work ~ The Invitation

This is where the story turns outward.
Everything I've learned, I now offer back:
Not as a guru.
Not as someone with all the answers.
But as someone who finally dared to live her questions out loud.

If you are looking for a place to begin again—my workshops
and courses were built for you.

For the one who left the faith but kept the ache.
For the mother trying to heal while raising someone else.
For the dreamer who was told it was too late.
If you are holding grief—release it.
If you are hiding your truth—speak it.
If you are afraid to choose yourself—do it afraid.

You get to rewrite the story.
And if you're reading this, it means you've already begun.

Start with a pause.
Take a deep breath . . . Exhale.

Now observe.

Your Next Step

If this book stirred something in you—
a memory, a question, a longing, a truth—
honor it.

Let this be more than a story you read.
Let it be the beginning of your return to yourself.

Join me in the spaces where healing takes root:
• **Rooted Reflections** workshops
• **Root to Rise** course
• Live conversations, guided journaling, and legacy work

Sign up to be the first to know about upcoming offerings, gatherings, and book updates:

You don't have to rise alone.
You don't have to bloom in silence.

We're growing through the concrete—together.

About the Author

Briana Cobb is an author, speaker, and advocate for personal liberation, mental wellness, and spiritual reclamation. After overcoming the compounded weight of childhood loss, religious conditioning, and systemic inequity, she found her voice in the stories she once felt silenced by.

Her debut memoir, Through the Concrete, is a deeply personal exploration of breaking cycles, reclaiming faith, and becoming whole on her own terms. Briana writes for those who have survived in silence, the daughter who had to be strong too soon, and the mother choosing a different path.

She is the founder of Na'Truely Crown'd, a holistic brand rooted in authenticity, healing, and empowerment. Through workshops, writing, and advocacy, Briana continues to help others grow through what they've been buried beneath.

She lives in Michigan with her husband and children and continues to use her story to plant seeds of courage in others— proving that even from the deepest pain, something beautiful can bloom.

www.ingramcontent.com/pod-product-compliance
Lightning Source LLC
Chambersburg PA
CBHW051517120626
46551CB00012B/965